MANAGE YOUR SUBSCRIPTION BUSINESS GROW YOUR CUSTOMER BASE

VIKRAM

Copyright 2019 by Vikram Ravishankaran

All rights reserved. No part of this book may be reproduced or transmitted in any form or by any means, electronic or mechanical including recording, photocopying, or by any information storage and retrieval system or devices, except in the case of brief quotations embodied in articles and reviews, without prior written permission of the publisher.

Although the author and publisher have made every effort to ensure the accuracy and completeness of information shared in this book, we assume no responsibility for errors, omissions, inaccuracies or any inconsistencies.

For more information, contact:

Vikram Ravishankaran

vikram.ravishankaran@gmail.com

Printed in the United States of America

DEDICATION

I would like to dedicate this book to my late grandfather for teaching me to read and write and shaping my career, my father and late mother for their love and support, my wife for always standing by me and having faith in everything I do, and my sweet daughter.

Table of Contents

FOREWORD	VI
PREFACE	X
ACKNOWLEDGEMENTS	XII
Chapter 1: OVERVIEW OF SUBSCRIPTION BUSINESS MODEL	1
Origin of Software as a Service (SaaS)	6
Cloud Computing	9
Public/Private Cloud	10
Understanding Order versus Subscription	13
Subscription Lifecycle Changes	15
Types of Subscription Orders	16
Editing Subscriptions	19
Cancellation of Subscriptions	22
Chapter 2: BENEFITS AND CHALLENGES	25
Benefits	26
Challenges	32
Chapter 3: WHY DO FEW SUBSCRIPTION-BASED COMPANIES FAIL?	37
Key Reasons	37
Chapter 4: CHOOSING THE RIGHT PRICING MODEL	45
Pricing Models	45
Pricing Strategies	46
Chapter 5: KNOW YOUR CUSTOMERS	59
Customer Bonding	59
Chapter 6: CUSTOMER RETENTION STRATEGIES	66
Managing Customer's Expectations	66

Customer Focus	69
Understanding Customer's Pulse and Giving them Irresistible Offers	70
Develop a Value Proposition	78
Believe in your Product	80
Advertise your Product	83
Reduce Customer Churn and Retain Customer Subscriptions	85
Charging for your Content	90
Early Termination	92
Chapter 7: REWARD YOUR CUSTOMERS	95
Reward Programs	95
Chapter 8: SUBSCRIPTION RENEWALS	104
Auto-Renewal Subscriptions	104
Manual Renewal Subscriptions	107
Effective Ways to Handle Subscription Renewal	111
Chapter 9: MEASURING THE PERFORMANCE OF YOUR SUBSCRIPTION BUSINESS	116
MRR Parameters	117
Chapter 10: SUCCESS STORIES	123
Conclusion	133

FOREWORD

This book is written in simple, easy to understand language. This book is a good starting point for any starry-eyed entrepreneur looking at starting a subscription-based business. It asks all the right questions, explains the key metrics that a potential entrepreneur should track and at the same time makes her aware of the potential pitfalls. Overall, a good speedy read which can be finished in one sitting and provides the necessary tools to an entrepreneur to test her business model with.

Neeraj Chhibba, Novelist of India's best-selling book "Zero Percentile"

Attracting capital has been a matter of concern for all the ventures since ages and in this generation of mushrooming start-ups one such innovation to appeal customer and investment is "Subscription Based Model" which has been elaborately discussed in this book. It provides insight into the types of subscription models, the benefits it bestows on the new entrepreneur and the way in which it should be improved, by maintaining trust and convenience in order to retain the customers. The illustrations provided and smooth language makes it really captivating for everyone who has ever been a customer to this subscription-based model as in this era where we have a lot to choose from an informed customer is the KING.

Noopur Choudhary, Head of Operations, OYO Indonesia

I find the book impressive and beneficial to any start-up company. Using realistic examples throughout the book helps readers relate to what you as a writer trying to convey. Vikram has executed that part incredibly well. This book also shows solid focus on customers, how to gain and retain them, and how to reward them. I liked his focus in the MRR section "measure your success is very critical". Using Cisco's subscription business model in the "success stories" sections is a great example of how Cisco took their business model to the next level. I highly recommend this book for new or established subscription-based companies.

-Monika Vondrka, Business Operations Manager, Cisco Systems, Inc.

This book acts as a comprehensive introduction to the subscription billing model. Vikram gives good advice for companies of all sizes to manage and retain customers. His use of anecdotes and analogies will help any reader digest and understand the concepts presented.

Michael McCarthy, Business Operations Analyst,
Cisco Systems, Inc.

In the times, when our everyday life has been impacted by one or the other subscription service. This book works as a guide to understand the subscription-based business models. It will be immensely useful for any upcoming startup which follows subscription-based model or any existing firm which want to compete in this space and offer its services as a subscription. Concepts explained are complemented with real life examples which makes it easier to comprehend and apply for an upcoming company.

-Atish Sharma, Strategy and Operations
Consultant, Deloitte India (Offices of the US)

Having known Vikram as a keen researcher and result-oriented individual, I feel that there are good take-aways from the book on topics about how to choose the right pricing model and why subscription-based companies fail. For me as an individual from networking background, understanding various reasons why business could fail is vital to launching a new subscription business in the right way and managing it then. I liked the examples that he has quoted throughout the book. They are very relatable. I highly recommend this book as a must-read for startups.

-Sudarshan Narasimhan, Principal Applications Engineer, Broadcom Inc.

The content in this book is very relatable to the reader which will give an extensive and comprehensive analysis on companies that are subscription based. Vikram has articulated his knowledge on must To-do's at scale for good customer relationships and retention strategies.

-Yxenia Contreras, Project Specialist, Cisco Systems, Inc.

PREFACE

In a world that has gone digital, we see start-ups and well-established companies shifting their business operational model to a subscription-based model and emerging as big players, we also see a few of them dropping out of the race for various reasons.

Subscription-based businesses can be very successful, but is it the right model for your business? What are the benefits and challenges of subscription-based model? Why do few subscription-based companies fail? Is your company's churn rate high? In other words, is the annual percentage at which customers stop subscribing to your product or service high? How can you choose the right pricing model for your business? How can you achieve the retention of existing customers? Where does most of the customer growth come from, is it from new customers or existing customers? How can you convert customers into loyal customers/members? What do you need to avoid your existing customers from quitting? How can you reward your loyal customers? How can you make your customers opt for renewal of subscription service? How can you measure the performance of your company?

This book has answers to all the above questions. Having learned and worked on subscription orders' end-to-end processing in IT projects for nearly 3 years, and having published 2 papers after research, I feel obliged to share my knowledge, observations, and tips that might be useful for managing subscription-based business that will eventually help in growing customer base and increasing sales productivity.

This book is targeted at startups and well-established subscription- based companies. I do not expect everyone to agree with the views and ideas shared in this book. I hope this book will give you a deeper understanding of the subscription-based model and drive higher rates of recurring revenue for your company by providing strategies to retain and reward loyal customers as well as acquire new customers.

ACKNOWLEDGEMENTS

I am very thankful to Neeraj Chhibba, Michael McCarthy, Monika Vondrka, Sudarshan Narasimhan, Yxenia Contreras, Atish Sharma, and Noopur Choudhary for taking their time to go through this book and for providing a foreword.

I would like to thank Greg Lim who reviewed the white paper that I published on a subscription-related topic last year and encouraged me to keep doing research and come up with more contributions.

I would like to extend my sincere gratitude to all my former and current supervisors, mentors, colleagues, and friends for their support and good wishes so far.

Chapter 1: OVERVIEW OF SUBSCRIPTION BUSINESS MODEL

This book is targeted at start-ups who have just migrated from the traditional on-premise perpetual model to subscription model and well-established companies to help them assess and improve customer retention and as well as get new customers. After going through this chapter, you will be able to understand how the subscription business model works, types of subscription orders, terms of subscription, high-level overview of SaaS and cloud computing.

When was the last time you saw a movie in a theater? How about the last time you watched a movie or show on Netflix, Hulu, or Amazon Prime? If you're like most customers, you have done the latter recently and you do it often.

Last week I was watching a TV series with my daughter on Netflix. We had finished viewing the first episode of the series, but I had to postpone the next episode till the next day as my wife and I have a set TV viewing time per day. In that moment I was thinking about how things have evolved and our adaptation to the changing times. During my childhood, I was hooked to quite a few TV series and had to wait for the next day or week to watch the next episode, we relied on fixed schedules set by media houses. We used to watch late-night TV shows which were live or repeat telecasts of the same show on the next day morning. Nowadays I can binge-watch any show on Netflix, thanks to the great content that Netflix has and the subscription model that made this possible. Welcome to the world of subscriptions.

With the access to a vast library of TV shows, movies, and original programs, Netflix has become very popular and successful through its online video streaming services. Netflix affects many industries, but the greatest impact is felt in film and TV. Even as movies bring in record amounts of money at the box office, Netflix grows its number of subscribers every year.

The Internet has dramatically revolutionized many different fields. It has become a global means of communication in our everyday lives.

Have you ever bought a gift for someone on a special occasion? How excited was the receiver? I am sure the receiver was excited, most people like surprises. What if you surprise them with a gift every 6 months for 3 years? You can make this happen through subscription. Think about how good it is to have something turn up on your doorstep, something you need, especially when you need it without having to think about it. One of the reasons why subscription businesses continue to be so successful is because of the element of surprise. People love to open a box without knowing what is inside. Subscription boxes give customers/members the opportunity to discover new brands and styles.

Even better, consider the thought of turning on your computer to find a software has new features, functionality, and bug fixes and then you then come to know of an upgrade that happened quietly over the weekend. Trust me, you will feel relieved knowing your time was not required during the upgrade. That is what subscription can offer. What is a subscription? You'll find out shortly.

A subscription business model is a model where a company sells a product or service to customers and in return receives recurring subscription revenue, be it monthly, quarterly, or yearly. Business-customer relationship no longer ends with the swipe of a credit card. In this model, end customers get regular deliveries of the product without any need for repeated searching or ordering. The goal is to create recurring revenue for many businesses.

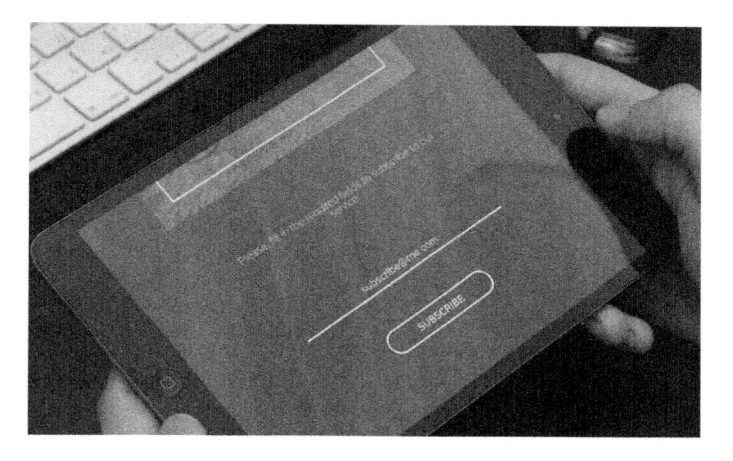

As long as your customers continually see the value your company provides for them, they will continually pay for the product (or) service.

Many businesses in various sectors like sports, movies, cosmetics, car leasing, traveling, furniture, shaving kit, streaming videos, music, fitness demos, dating, cooking manuals and consumer goods use subscription models. With the increase in the number of subscription companies, I have noticed a larger shift from the product economy to the subscription economy.

Subscription also creates economies, retains customers, and simplifies many business processes, making them easier in the end. Managing a subscription company means there is a continuing relationship with the customer. For example, the customer may purchase a one-year subscription to enter a sports activities community with preliminary access to the gym at a fixed price.

Customers may pay the entire sum upfront or pay on a monthly basis. The subscription model can be applied for various businesses, including magazines, cable services, newspapers, clubhouse, and any business that provides recurring products or services. What may be surprising to some is that organizations offering a recurring product have been around for several years. Daily/weekly shipping of newspaper and milk have been around for many years.

Subscription-based models have managed to spread in many business areas. But there is still a great scope of improvement for the utilization of subscription-based models in different business areas.

Subscription-based models allow customers to hop-on, renew, upgrade, downgrade, or discontinue a service anytime they want. This helps them understand if new products and services suit them and provide them the flexibility to explore new products and services.

For instance, health care providers get recurring income every month that helps them focus on better delivery. Subscriptions allow patients to access healthcare services at affordable rates by paying recurring fees according to the preference of the customer, be it monthly, quarterly, or yearly. It also helps in improving the relationship with customers and bringing them to the retention point sooner, leading to membership growth.

Before we discuss the positive impact that the subscription model has had on the way many subscription-based companies operate, it is important that you understand about Subscription SaaS and cloud computing at a high level. It will help you to understand why the subscription model is becoming a favorite over the traditional on-premise delivery model.

Origin of Software as a Service (SaaS)

Since the 1990s, the internet has enormously affected the business culture. At the leap forward of the thousand years, the Dot Com happened. This was the emergency of trust. IT merchants expected to recapture the trust and enthusiasm of speculators, so they began to consider building up another plan of action. That is how cloud computing came into the picture.

When talking about software as a Service (SaaS) and cloud computing, people tend to use the two terms interchangeably. Although the two technologies are related, they are not the same. Alright then, let us find how they differ. SaaS is a type of cloud computing that offers additional services like Platform as a Service (PaaS) and Infrastructure as a Service (IaaS). Both SaaS and cloud computing are delivered via internet technologies and offer similar benefits to users.

SaaS is ideally suited to cloud computing and applications that run on any desktop or mobile device, regardless of the operating system. Applications are maintained within the provider's data center. When software upgrades are done, it is reflected in all the users accessing the services at once. Users launch their browsers or apps and go online and they get the newest version, there is no need to install or upgrade software locally. Differences between SaaS and On-Premise model have been listed in below table.

SaaS	On-Premise
SaaS is accessed via the	On-premise

internet. It is not installed and maintained through company hard drives.	implementation is a cumbersome process. It features in-house installation.
SaaS offers a variety of advantages over traditional software licensing models. As the software is not present on the licensing company's servers, there is less or no demand for the company to invest in new hardware.	The IT department takes care of the maintenance of the server and software upgrade.
It is easier to take care of software implementation, perform regular updates, and debug issues, if any. Implementation requires lower upfront cost. Multiple software licenses are not required, even if there	For large organizations, updating software is a time-consuming process. Software updates are available for download through the internet, with companies purchasing additional licenses rather than additional disks. Copies of the software

will be multiple computers.	are installed on all the other devices that need access.
SaaS is hosted by a provider and can be accessed with a browser and Wi-Fi network. SaaS provides more opportunities to use the software irrespective of location. This is suitable for employees who travel often or work from home.	On-premise can only be accessed on the company network only.

Cloud Computing

I am sure you have heard the phrase, "We are moving to the cloud". What does that mean?

Cloud computing is a utility service that gives on-demand access to technology resources managed by experts. It is computing in which large groups of remote servers are networked to enable centralized data storage and online access to computer services and resources. Businesses built around cloud computing are called SaaS.

These offerings can be simply accessed over the internet with no upfront costs, you only pay for the resources you use. Innovation has changed the manner in which business works, making processing power increasingly accessible and practical, and routinely outperforming past execution benchmarks. With the innovation of new products and services, IT has turned into a business enablement machine. Businesses are connecting with customers by means of informal communities, analyzing data trends, and developing new must-have products and services by making use of the power of cloud computing.

To summarize, cloud computing has the following significant benefits.

- Lower cost of ownership
- Easily upgradable
- Always up
- Disaster maintenance
- Productivity anywhere
- Offsite data storage
- No IT maintenance costs

Public/Private Cloud

Public and private cloud are different models of cloud computing. Public clouds are internet-based computing that allow the on-demand sharing of software, resources, and data. With Private cloud, only a limited number of approved users can access the data. A private cloud hosting solution resides on a company's intranet or hosted data center where data is protected behind a firewall.

Users of internally managed clouds have full control and responsibility for their data. Users who want the security of the private cloud model also have a third option, a (third-party) managed private cloud. These private clouds are cloud infrastructures operated by third-party providers.

I have listed the main differences between private cloud and public cloud in the table below for your quick reference.

Public Cloud	Private Cloud
Data is stored in the provider's data center and the provider is responsible for the management and maintenance of the data center.	Management, maintenance, and updating of data centers is the responsibility of the company. Few companies see this as a

	drawback as it consumes time.
It might seem as though it's insecure, but all your data remains separate from others and security breaches are rare.	There is increased level of security.
Variable cost for additional capacity	On-demand scalability
No guaranteed resources	Guaranteed resources
Preferred for smaller businesses	Preferred for large companies
Lesser control over data	Better control over data
Appealing to many companies as lead time in testing and deploying new products is reduced.	Deploying new products consumes time in testing and the company takes responsibility for it.

It is indeed very hard for any company to resist moving their data to a Cloud infrastructure. The best cloud providers have hundreds of experts available to support the IT strategies and meet the hardware, software licensing, operating system, data protection, and disaster recovery requirements.

The cloud provider frees IT staff from performing hardware maintenance and operating systems upgrades. This rescued time frees up IT to specialize in innovation, or it will solve employees hiring and retention issues.

Cloud manages risk by reducing downtime, improving application performance, and meeting compliance regulations. IT project backlogs and time-to-service are minimized by reducing the keep-the-lights-on IT maintenance work. This helps finance teams by accurately quantifying the incremental costs of specific projects. Current problem in hiring and retaining IT infrastructure employees is addressed.

It is very important that you connect the dots from business requirements to IT projects, so all departments can clearly see the benefits of subscription model and cloud computing.

Understanding Order versus Subscription

Many people tend to use the two terms order and subscription interchangeably, but they are not one and the same. An order submitted by a customer or agent on behalf of a customer is the "transaction" that leads to the creation of a subscription (agreement between Company and Customer) to provide services for a certain fee/price. Subscription is the continuation of this contract. It captures the latest status of relationship and further changes that could be incurred. Most of the functions listed in the below flow diagram in general will be part of subscription-based company's order flow.

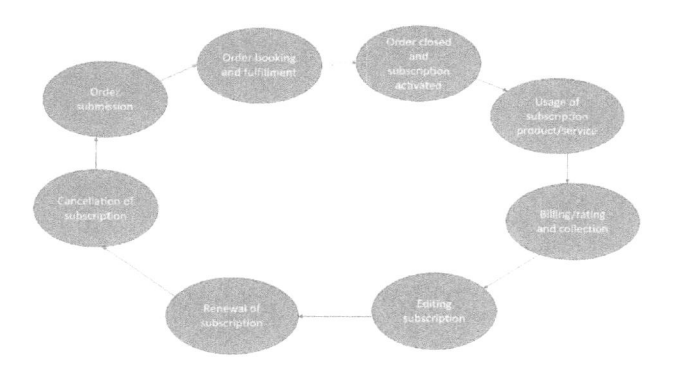

Order: Subscription Relationship

After reading this section, you will be able to understand the different types of subscription, the life cycle of subscriptions, editing subscriptions, and cancelling of subscriptions. One order can have multiple subscriptions, many orders can also link to one subscription. Orders could be a new order, change order – add/replace/remove, cancel subscription order, or an auto-renewal order.

Subscription Lifecycle Changes

1. **Change subscriptions:** Customer wants to upsell or down-sell the subscription.
2. **Stop auto-renewal:** Customer decides to stop auto-renewal on a subscription that was originally configured with the auto-renewal option.
3. **Mid-term cancellation:** This is initiated by partners or customers for prepaid and recurring billing subscriptions.
4. **Subscription transfer:** Customer transfers subscription from one partner to another partner.
5. **Subscription migration:** Subscription is moved from one billing platform to another platform.

Let us go through the different terms of subscription below.

Initial Term

This is the duration (in months) for the initial committed term of the subscription.

Renewal Term

This is the duration (in months) for the auto-renewal term of a subscription. A customer with auto-renewal enabled will continue to have their initial term extended unless they submit a change-replace order. Renewal term period could be for 6 months or 1 year in general.

Grace Period

When a customer does not enable auto-renewal, the grace period is the window after expiration (typically 60 days) in which customer can get their original subscription re-activated.

Prepayment Term

Prepayment term is the number of months the customer agrees to pay in advance. Prepayment term will drop to whatever the current term is. Once the subscription starts, the billing cycle is activated.

Let us read and understand the various types of subscription orders.

Types of Subscription Orders

New Subscription Order

Let's say for instance you subscribe to the internet connection of Xfinity, the telephone service company. In case you are not aware, they market consumer cable television, internet, telephone, and wireless services provided by the company. This new connection to Xfinity will be treated as a new subscription. You may make the payment recurring or manual for the bills that Xfinity will send you on a monthly basis.

From the perspective of a subscription offer, say a customer wants to purchase a recurring cloud or subscription or software product from your company, a new subscription will be created for the customer. The customer will be able to select their initial term, renewal term, billing model, and requested start date.

The variations made available to the customer can be restricted at the product level. The customer can select any valid combination of products under their chosen subscription product. Subscription code will stay the same throughout the course of this subscription. If the billing model is annual, bills will be sent each year.

Auto-Renewal

Customers can choose a renewal term (maximum 12 months) at the time of their initial purchase. Subscription code will stay the same between both subscriptions.

Transfer/Migration

Occasionally, services need to be transferred or migrated to a different subscription. For example, if a customer wants to move from one partner to another partner due to better support that other partner might provide, or two customers have completed a merger and want to combine their subscriptions.

If the subscription is already on the latest platform, the existing subscription can be cancelled, and the services transferred to a new account.

Expiration/Manual Renewal

When auto-renewal is not enabled for a subscription product, in order to continue receiving services from a company, the customer/partner must enter a manual renew order.

If a manual renewal order is not submitted or fulfilled before the expiration of the subscription term, the customer will experience a service interruption.

Subscription code will stay the same between both subscriptions. A customer has until the end of the grace period to recover their original subscription code and after that, a new order must be placed.

Editing Subscriptions

Assuming you have not come across subscriptions, or have limited knowledge of how they work, let me explain in a simpler way. During my childhood days, my parents had subscribed to receive the newspaper daily. I developed an interest in reading comics books when I started going to high school, so we ordered for comics books to be delivered once a week along with the newspaper. This is what editing a subscription is all about.

Basically, a change was done to the original subscription order in order to accommodate the delivery of a new product in addition to the initial product being delivered. You are free to decide your own frequency of delivery of the product. A customer with an existing subscription can make a change, for example, increase or decrease the quantity of products, change the billing schedule, billing model, or subscription's requested start date.

Once I started going to college, I started involving myself in outdoor activities related to sports. We discontinued getting comics books from the store and continued to receive only the newspaper. This is also an example of subscription change where a product was removed from the original subscription order.

The subscription code will stay the same throughout the course of this subscription. The good news is that existing customers are much easier to sell to. But if it's so much easier to sell to your existing customers than acquire new ones, why do so many subscription model-based companies struggle in this area?

You want to upsell to a customer at a time when they have a need for your additional features – a time when upgrading makes sense to them. Keep a track of success milestones of the customer and look out for logical opportunities to expand the business. This is the best upselling opportunity.

For example, if the mobile family plan has a limit of 5 users, when the 5th person joins the plan, you have reached the limit of the number of users permitted on your basic plan. Sticking with this plan will limit the value they get from it, so it's a very good opportunity to reach out to that customer and offer them the chance to upgrade. If your customer will benefit from upsell, take the required action for the same.

The most important thing to remember is that upselling to your customers should never be random, you need to focus on the customer rather than your service. What does your customer need from your subscription product? How would the upsell help your customer to do better and achieve her goals?

Does the customer's existing usage of your subscription product suggest she would get an appropriate level of value from the upsell?

It's very easy to focus your communication with the customer on your product, when in fact, your focus should be on how it will benefit her.

You may develop customizations in your IT systems to allow a subscription product to be replaced with some other subscription product. When that happens, an existing subscription gets deactivated and a new subscription is created in the system.

Cancellation of Subscriptions

I am sure you have cancelled at least one of these connections – internet service, phone service, Netflix, HBO, a connection to video streaming service. Why did you cancel the subscriptions? I am sure it was because you found better content or products for a better price with some other company.

If you are hearing that customers do not like what you are offering them, it is likely the right time to take their feedback seriously and make some improvements.

If you cannot gain much insight by studying the cancellation pattern and reading ex-customers' comments about your products, your company is likely to keep making the same mistake again with some other customers. I am not talking about people who experienced a free trial of your product and did not subscribe, I am talking about customers who have been using your product for a few months/years and then cancelled their subscription.

They liked your product or service, but something made them change their mind. You need to know what that something was. Conduct a survey of the people who have already canceled and find out why. Most of them will be happy to tell you the reason behind the cancellation.

Also, make sure to ask them if they will recommend the product to a friend? It is possible that some of the customers liked your subscription product and did not have any issue with it, but they had to unsubscribe/cancel the subscription due to reasons such as financial crunch, they might be the wrong audience, or might have had a personal reason. These customers might recommend to their friends, family or colleague citing they might find it useful. On fewer occasions, certain customers cancel their subscription and come back later. Overall, at the end of the survey, you will be able to rank the top 5 reasons why they cancelled. This will help to watch the behavior of current customers and predict what they are about to do.

Many enterprise software companies have been shifting their business model from on-premise perpetual pricing model to subscription license-based software-as-a-service (SaaS). There are many long-term benefits in the form of business growth, lesser infrastructure support, and administration. At the same time, there are challenges faced in the sustenance of the business in a subscription-based model. Let us read and find out the benefits and challenges of subscription business model in next chapter.

Chapter 2: BENEFITS AND CHALLENGES

After going through this chapter, you will be able to understand the benefits and challenges of a subscription business model. I'll restrain from mentioning the areas that need attention as cons of the subscription model as they are not pitfalls. After reading this section, you will have a good idea if the subscription business model is a route that might work for you.

Have you come across below?

On a scale of 0 to 10 where 0 = Not at all Satisfied and 10 = Extremely Satisfied.

- How satisfied are you with the mobile representative(s) you spoke with?
- How easy was it for you to resolve your issue?
- How satisfied are you with the ability of the representatives to fix your issue?

You would have probably given 10 when your issue was resolved sooner by the customer representative and would have given lesser than 5 in case of poor customer experience.

Yes, customer experience is the next competitive battleground. Customers like doing business with an organization that provides quality service. It has become a common practice for customers to make one-off purchases from organizations just for the sake of discounts and promotional offers. It is difficult to have interaction and develop long-term relationships with customers in a short period. But with the monthly/yearly nature of subscription services, you have an extended period to develop a long-term relationship with your customer.

You get to know what they value and the change they like to see in the services provided. Their feedback will enable you to additionally improve your model and retain customers for the long term. Good customer relationship will help increase business during these social media-driven times. Customers who like your products and services are most likely to share a positive feedback with their friends and colleagues. Customer service is one part of the customer experience, but it has a large impact on the overall experience.

Benefits

Subscription-Based Pricing

I am sure you know how down payment works in real estate. Many homebuyers make down payments of 5% to 25% of the total value of the home, and a bank or other financial institution will cover the remainder of the costs through a mortgage loan. It is tough to even dream of buying something expensive if the concept of the mortgage loan was not in existence. Having said that, it is indeed a win-win situation for banks, real estate owners, and customers. Let us move to the subscription world and take a similar example.

Charging customers $50 per month is more attractive than charging them $1000 in one go. This is because the higher price is a barrier to entry for your products. Subscription-based pricing attracts more customers. There are exceptions, but in general, the more expensive your product is, the fewer customers it will attract.

Subscription payments lower the barrier to entry for product and services and permit additional potential customers to buy your product. While customers may pay a larger amount over the long term, they can get immediate access to the product. Customers additionally relish the increased features you'll give as your company's business grows and you improve your product over time.

Since you are not impacted by the cost of shipping products and may have the flexibility to accept all kinds of payments, global markets are easier to reach. Even within the case of enterprise deals, the lower price could allow you to fly under the threshold budget and assist you avoid long sales negotiations with procurement teams. This promotes the growth of your monthly recurring revenue (MRR).

In the subscription-based pricing model, customers pay on a regular basis for a service or product. Subscription pricing is different than pricing for traditional products, as pricing is often based on the length of the subscription, making longer subscriptions the cheapest options.

Predictable Revenue

One of the quick wins of the subscription model is that your company's income can be well predicted on a month to month basis. The subscription business model will have a great impact on your business.

One of the best things about any recurring revenue stream is dependable income. This suggests, you will be able to budget additional exactly, make reliable projections, and plan to have certain amounts of raw materials and finished inventory in stock. Having a solid subscription system in place makes those buying cycles far less stressful.

Unlike a company that sells thousands of products whose popularity depends on a variety of factors, subscription services sell a single product that is guaranteed to the buyer, and in return, the buyer guarantees their payment.

With subscription business model, customers make payment to you on a regular basis. Since the amount of recurring payments is decided on at the time of initial sale, it allows you to predict your revenue each month. This conjointly ensures that you simply aren't ordering additional supplies or stocking more inventory than you would like.

With billing automation for recurring billing, there are fewer gaps between billing cycles. This helps plug revenue leakages. There is an upfront cost of trying to reach and win over new customers (as with all businesses), but once those customers are in and sign up for your service, you can predict revenue for months in advance and breathe a little sigh of relief.

Strong Customer Relationships

If you are in the subscription business, you are in the customer service business. Customer-first is the best approach when you're using the subscription business model. Strong customer relationships are at the core of the subscription business model. It is hard to achieve recurring revenue without strong customer relationships. Developing deep relationships with your customers is crucial to increasing your customer base.

While acquiring new customers is of high priority, changes to existing subscriptions like renewals, upgrades, cancellations/terminations constitute the vast majority of customer transactions in the subscription economy. Building on existing customer relationships is much less resource-intensive than acquiring new customers. Ideally, you should have a 24/7 support service, as well as a customer service support team. Closely monitor the customer usage and adoption to mitigate churn risk. A stable, happy customer base is essential to continuous growth.

More Earnings Through Up and Cross-Selling

Upsells are usually easier in a subscription-based business when you have a good relationship with your customer. Your customer will be receptive to any added value you can provide to them. Maintaining continuous contact with your customers builds a strong bond of trust. This makes it easier to market extra and complementary offerings to them.

Additionally, once subscription fees become a part of the expected monthly or annual budget of customers, it becomes easier for them to see additional features as more affordable. This is especially true for customers using your subscription to learn and/or grow, they may find that add-ons enable them to achieve goals more efficiently.

Various pricing models like tiered pricing, volume pricing, etc. can allow customers to easily move up the upgrade path when they are ready.

Potential for Untapped Markets

One of the things that have opened the door for success for subscription providers is their ability to consider and pursue untapped markets. If you take Netflix or Amazon Prime for example, they have forever changed the way movies could be rented and watched. Due dates, late fees, and hefty rental prices per movie became a thing of the past when Netflix turned DVD rentals into a subscription service in the early 2000s.

Another example I would like to take is the razor industry which Gillette ruled for several years. With that famous and innovative YouTube video, Dollar shave club made a good entry into razor industry. They have mastered the art of upsell with their entry into toothpaste, face lotion subscriptions. Subscription-based companies have the potential to enter untapped markets in the industry and become leaders.

Lower Budget for Customer Retention

Due to the nature of subscription services, you can spend far less on customer retention. Although it is true that you need to focus on making sure your customers continue to be pleased with your product and services, they are guaranteed to give revenue to your business through their purchase. You don't need constant marketing and encouragement for them to come back and purchase again from your company. There is no guarantee that customers will stay forever but there is a great possibility that they will stay and opt for upgraded or extra subscription services rather than continuing with the same services.

Challenges

In this section, you will learn the challenges of a subscription business model.

Risk of High Cancellation or Termination

Churn, or cancellation, is one of the biggest risks of subscription-based companies. There is some reliability for your income when a customer signs up. But what will be the driving factor for them to stay or continue their partnership with you? More importantly, what is going to prevent them from cancelling or terminating the subscription?

It is important to anticipate this risk. It is also important to look at the bigger picture and develop a good rapport with customers and take care of their changing needs from time to time. Extra fees and cancellations should be handled with care. Termination is always a risk. On fewer occasions, certain customers discontinue opting for subscription services and later come back again. So, you would prefer not to stoke the fire by having negative discussions with customers when they leave you the first time.

Reluctancy to Commit

From cable service to gym memberships, signing a contract can make customers a little nervous and they might get a second thought. There is the danger of realizing you have agreed to something in the beginning, but you end up thinking if you want it or not afterwards. There is the risk of not having the money you thought you had to pay for it.

For a variety of reasons, people can have commitment issues when it comes to signing a contract. Due to this, it can be hard to sell customers on a subscription service. It feels like a huge commitment. Therefore, the front-end customer procurement budget is important. You have to convince your customers that it is worth the commitment and it will improve their business and boost their revenue, making it worth the extra cost.

Data Security

As a subscription-based company, you will be storing customers' sensitive details such as phone number, email address, billing address and shipping address in your system. So, it is your company's responsibility to make sure all your customers' data is handled safely and will never be shared with anyone other than the customer. Your company needs to keep looking for opportunities to make improvements and provide a highly secure, scalable system with a great subscription and billing experience to their customers.

Once customers terminate their subscription, company should return all the sensitive details to customer. This is one of the biggest sticking points for companies that are considering the subscription model as their business model. Security is an important consideration when allowing company/subscription-based vendors to maintain your business-critical data, especially for companies with critical data.

In reality, data security is independent of whether the server is on your premises or in a different city.

Web-based systems have more security measures in place than on-premise systems and have started to invest more money in security, backups, and maintenance.

For instance, with Amazon webservices, they have put strong safeguards in place to help protect customer privacy. All data is stored in highly secure AWS data centers. Irrespective of size of your business, the AWS infrastructure is designed to keep data safe.

Product Offerings

Customers can lose enthusiasm for a product on the off chance that it doesn't change, develop, or overhaul at incessant interims. On the off chance that customers begin to feel like they are simply accepting old news consistently, they may very well lose intrigue and proceed onward. With services like Amazon Prime and Netflix, new shows and movies are added and removed each month. This creates some curiosity among viewers or users. Even if you offer a single product, there are N number of approaches that your company can follow to make sure that the service remains unique that is worth customers' investment.

System Availability

With a monthly subscription service, all your customers are getting the same service every month, at about the same time. This improves the procedure, generally, yet it can turn out to be extra upsetting on the off chance that you keep running into hiccups. Ongoing maintenance of subscription-based company's systems and services is done with ease. It is good to see some of the enterprise technology companies selling infrastructure services on subscription basis. But, a small glitch in the system could mean you get behind on every single order at once and delivery of the planned shipments could get delayed. Additional downtime can lead to longer delays in shipments of the order resulting in customer dissatisfaction.

With so many customers, it can be difficult to notice single or few transactions that have failed during system's availability issues. But, subscription-based companies need to make sure that notifications of failed transactions are sent to customers especially when system is not available (or) having a glitch.

To summarize, benefits such as flexibility in pricing, lesser system availability issues when compared to traditional on-premise delivery model, flexibility in consumption of subscription services, ability to make more earnings through upselling and cross-selling, good data security plans, ability and flexibility to manage costs, regular review of pricing models are definitely driving customers towards subscription-based model. But you still see some subscription-based companies failing. Isn't it? Let us discuss on this topic in the following chapter.

Chapter 3: WHY DO FEW SUBSCRIPTION-BASED COMPANIES FAIL?

After reading this chapter, you will have a good idea of where few subscription-based companies go wrong. It will help you when you try to launch a new subscription-based company (or) with better management of your existing business.

Key Reasons

Key reasons why subscription-based companies fail are as follows.

High Churn Rate

Most startup companies operate like any other online venture and within no time realize they are not getting breakthrough in the business. Churn is unavoidable for any subscription-based business. When your company isn't offering a service different from what the competition is offering, you are not adding any value. Customers expect to get a product far more valuable than what they are paying for or they will be switching over to competitors in no time.

If your company does not have a clear vision of your expected customer base, your business is most likely to fail. By defining your target customers, you can better determine if there are enough potential customers for your business. In general, there will not be much of a difference in products between competitors. 75% of customers are likely to switch companies/brands because of a poor customer experience. After one negative experience, 50% of customers will never do business with a company again. If you do not tailor your products and services to better meet your customers' needs, they are likely to cancel the subscription or not renew the services. Branding is important because it makes a memorable impression on customers and also allows them to know what to expect from your company. Target your marketing efforts to reach your most promising prospects.

Start-up companies sometimes resist defining a target customer base, thinking it might limit the business or reduce the number of potential customers. This is a misconception. Identifying target customers does not prevent your business from accepting customers that don't fit the target profile.

To have a working business model, startup companies need to find ways to increase the lifetime value of a customer while keeping the cost of acquiring the customer down. For any subscription-based company to break even, the churn rate should remain constant as customer growth increases. When churn (customer turnover) is greater than growth (customer acquisition rate), the business will fail. This is why subscription-based companies need to focus on keeping churn as low as possible. It is possible that your highest churn is likely coming from your low-tier plan customers. This can impact your future acquisition as well. So, keep a close eye on MRR churn and customer retention rate and find opportunities to optimize your product as required. In one of the upcoming chapters, I will walk you through Churn MRR and customer retention rate with examples.

Also, there are business management issues that could prevent a subscription-based company from succeeding. Initial market penetration is exceptionally hard. New customers will not believe in your product as it does not have creditability. Getting the initial set of customers is challenging.

So, you have to educate the customers about your product and tell them what problem you are trying to solve.

Finding and meeting investors can be a challenge on its own, before having to convince them to actually invest. Feeling like you deserve investors' attention and money and that it is unjust that you aren't getting it is a very common sentiment among many entrepreneurs. Make sure you have multi-channel support and fine-tune your user flow in such a way that customer acquisition process is simple and requires lesser manual intervention.

No Value Addition to Customers

Most subscription-based businesses fail because they are simply not solving any existing problem. Others may be solving a problem that customers do not want solved.

The only way out is adding value to the product or service offered by your competitors. How do you add value? You can find customers' pain points related to that product or service through regular customer connects and surveys. As your competitors make the move to promote their business, you can learn from both their successes and their failures while you are working on your own product development and marketing strategies. Addressing the problems that current industry players or competitors are facing is a good start and will help you capture the market.

The cash flow of sponsors plays a significant role. On-boarding of customers is becoming easier with automation. This will help to scale up your customer base, although it's not easy. This is also a source of failure for subscription-based companies. To build, specific business strategies are necessary.

So, your company has been around for a year or two now, and you think you have reached product/market fit. Things look good as long as people use your product. When customers use your product, you will get to know their feedback and of bugs if any. Solving a problem that customers report in a swift manner will help grow your customer base. As a subscription-based company, keep focusing on continuous product and service improvement.

Unfocused Growth

Most subscription-based companies tend to be technology and product-focused. Having said that, I agree it is difficult to achieve product/market fit without core technical expertise and product development skills. If demos/free trials do not convert into customer subscriptions, many companies come up with a way to add new features and make the product better.

Likewise, subscription-based companies tend to work on developing new features if they are not attracting enough visitors to their website, getting enough attention, or if customers are not giving good business. This works to some extent but will only drive incremental growth, not the exponential growth your company really needs when it reaches product/market fit to swallow up the market. What is the option you have here?

Poor Marketing

It is not enough to just keep improving your product anymore, customers have already indicated that they will buy your product as it stands. How will you as a company achieve this? Sit down to think and develop a sales and marketing strategy as you cannot just rely on your great product alone to sell itself. Where do you start? Hire a sales team which can help in marketing, build an in-house sales marketing team, and partner with marketing experts to develop and implement aspects of your marketing strategy.

Great products have failed because of poor marketing. Failure of a business is mainly due to bad marketing, lack of understanding of product positioning and demographic miscalculation. So, all you need to do is to have a good marketing team that will keep a watch on ever-changing customer needs and market trends and help your business grow.

Being successful at this stage means acquiring customers as quickly as possible. It is likely that your existing customers will not be able to support your customer acquisition costs for new customers if you are growing rapidly. That means you will need a lot of funding. Once new customers are acquired, continuous success or growth is guaranteed. Develop a serious sales and marketing strategy, raise funding, and get those customers in through the door.

Incorrect Pricing Strategies

If you do not revisit and review the pricing model that your company needs to adopt, you are heading for trouble. If you charge your customers too much, you will alienate your customers and price yourself out of the market. As your product or service improves over time, you should vary your pricing to track the value you provide. Failing to decide your subscription pricing of product or service could lead you to overprice or underprice your product or services. There is a risk of losing customers due to high-pricing. If you don't charge enough, you'll run the risk of undermining your own business and sinking under the cost of running it.

Deciding how much to charge your customers shouldn't be taken lightly, and yet many companies simply don't give it enough thought. Your pricing model must be reviewed at regular intervals. However, if you don't adopt the correct pricing model, it really does not matter how much you charge because your customers won't sign up in the first place. You have to find the correct model that suits your customers' needs and helps to grow your company.

Choosing the right pricing model is crucial to the success of your business. Let me walk you through the various pricing models that will give you an idea of how to choose the right one for your business.

Chapter 4: CHOOSING THE RIGHT PRICING MODEL

Many enterprise software companies have been shifting their business model from on-premise – perpetual pricing model to subscription license-based software-as-a-service (SaaS). There are many long-term benefits in the form of business growth, lesser infrastructure support, and administration. At the same time, there are challenges faced in the sustenance of the business in a subscription-based model. On an average, startups spend just six hours on their pricing strategy. That's not six hours a week, or six hours a month - six hours, ever, to define, test, and optimize everything.

Many startups try to make high profits in a short span of time and eventually run out of business due to incorrect choice of pricing model. Choosing the right pricing model is key to a successful transition. After going through this chapter, you will be able to understand how to assess and choose the correct pricing model for your company. Failure to capture the right price not only eliminates the profits but also damages the market, especially when a company gives too many high discounts. Let us read about various pricing models that are out there.

Pricing Models

Pricing model requires high-level strategic initiatives that will ultimately determine if a company thrives or goes out of business. Take a SaaS pricing model for example, they typically bill customers using one of the following two metrics:

1) The number of users

2) The volume of resources consumed

Most of the applications adopt pay per user and pay-as-you-go pricing models. They use monthly, quarterly, and yearly billing models.

Billing Models

This identifies the frequency at which the invoices will be generated for recurring charges. Subscription-based businesses must be able to adapt and adjust to the ever-changing economic climate of e-commerce and the customers whom they work with. Digital businesses can easily monetize the entire customer lifecycle and initiate growth with recurring revenue.

Pricing Strategies

A pricing strategy is a method used to establish the best price for a product or service. There is no single strategy that is applicable for every customer base and their business. While one subscription option may be a great fit for one company, it will be disastrous for another company. It is important to consider the needs and preferences of your target audience as well as the budget for your business.

Companies spend a lot of effort in making a product and bringing in new customers, but companies must improve how to communicate a product's worth to customers. Companies spend countless hours improving their product, tweaking their positioning, and acquiring new customers. Yet, most subscription companies spend little time thinking about their pricing. Create a process for reviewing your company's pricing models every six months.

Understand the customer first and come up with a pricing strategy. If you do not come up with a good pricing strategy, you are missing the opportunity to grow your revenue exponentially.

Growth is more revenue and not just more customers. Choose the right pricing model.

Pricing is a great growth opportunity. When you optimize your pricing, your company becomes more efficient. To know if your business is making profits, you need to know these parameters. The ratio between lifetime value per customer and customer acquisition costs has to be more than 1. If not, you are losing some money per customer. If this ratio is lesser than 1, it means growth is slower. In addition to focusing on customer acquisition, focus on having regular pricing reviews in your company. Revisions to pricing value can help your company in high revenue growth. After reading the section below, you will be able to understand various types of pricing models that are available for use.

1) Tiered User Pricing

In the case of tiered user pricing, the number of permitted users increases in bands rather than single digits. For example, a SaaS product may cost one price for up to 5 users, another price from 5 to 10 users, and so on.

Providers who use this pricing model typically include increasing number of features or types of functionality within each successive tier. It is easier to see how it works using an example.

Say, pricing of gadgets has been setup as below.

- 01-20 = $100 per gadget
- 21-30 = $90 per gadget
- 31-40 = $80 per gadget
- 41+ = $75 per gadget

Cost Breakdown

Say, you have sold 45 gadgets:

- First 20 gadgets cost $100 each
- Next 10 gadgets cost $90 each
- Next 10 gadgets cost $80 each
- Additional 5 gadgets cost $75 each

Total cost = (20 * 100) + (10 * 90) + (10 * 80) + (5 * 75)

Total cost = $4075

2) Volume Pricing

In volume pricing, same price is defined for all units within the range. It's easier to see how it works using an example. Let's say the pricing of gadgets has been setup as below.

- 01-20 = $100 per gadget
- 21-30 = $90 per gadget
- 31-40 = $80 per gadget
- 41+ = $75 per gadget

Cost Breakdown

Let's say you have sold 45 gadgets:

- Total cost = (45 * 75)

Total cost = $3375

Volume pricing, on the other hand, means that as soon as you hit a particular number, all units will cost the lower price. The flow chart below shows the comparative study between volume and tiered pricing using the above example.

Volume vs Tiered pricing

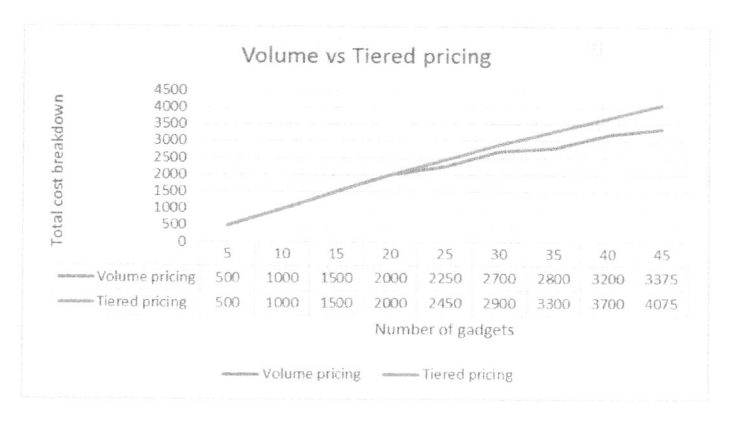

	5	10	15	20	25	30	35	40	45
Volume pricing	500	1000	1500	2000	2250	2700	2800	3200	3375
Tiered pricing	500	1000	1500	2000	2450	2900	3300	3700	4075

Number of gadgets

The main difference between tiered and volume pricing is that tiered pricing increases the reach to your potential audience because you are offering different pricing versions for your product. Customers will pay up to what they can afford. New customers will opt for lower price plans first and may eventually switch over to higher-priced plans. To be innovative, you may package products and service together and sell in the tiered pricing.

3) Pay-Per-User

Pay-per-user is a popular pricing strategy. In this model, a separate cost is incurred for each user of a SaaS application. It is similar to paying for each copy of the software. The advantage over traditional software pricing is that SaaS is available on almost all devices and does not usually incur separate charges for tablets, laptops, phones, and other devices. Subscription-based billing occurs on a periodic basis (usually monthly) for all the registered users. It can hurt some companies where the number of individual users is high.

Per-user pricing is worth considering if subscribers frequently start small but increase their users significantly over time – in this case, per-user pricing attracts new subscribers with a low initial price. It is possible to capture more revenue from each subscriber as they derive value from your offering and add more users.

A variation of the pay-per-user pricing model is the pay-per-multiple-user pricing model, wherein a separate cost is incurred for a specified number of users. To understand why per-user pricing is not good for most SaaS products, you first need to review the concept of a SaaS pricing value metric. Remember, a "value metric" is what and how you're charging for a product or service. Say, your company is selling laptops, then your value metric is measured in terms of days, your company laptops served the customers without a crash. Likewise, the subscription product must be easy for customers to understand. Subscription service must meet the customers' expectations. With time, value metrics will grow higher as customers' usage increases.

If you conduct a survey and ask which value metrics are most and least preferred, you will see that value is seen in additional sales, contacts, reports, and the number of users is the least preferred value metrics. This is not to suggest that users should not be a part of your model anymore, but it should not be your primary value metric, especially if you are selling a marketing or analytics product. Even then, you need to have product differentiation to push for customer pricing segmentation and to make customers feel curious about what upgraded features are present in the premium version.

4) Freemium Model

Let the customers experience your product or service with a free plan – Freemium model. Once the customers start using your products and services, they will realize the potential and benefit of that product and may think of upgrading to a paid plan. One good example of a freemium model is Candy Crush, a mobile app game with optional in-app purchases. You will be able to play the game for free, but you will get a better experience if you become a paid customer. Take a software that does the conversion of files from word format (.doc) or an image file (.jpeg) to a PDF file for example, most of us have the need to use this software occasionally.

As part of the freemium mode, it lets the guest users to do the file conversion of a word document or image file of smaller size. A message "Sign up for a subscription at $20 per year and convert files of unlimited size" gets popped up. It is a good idea to popup a message for customers saying conversion will be 10x faster if they sign up for subscription. Some of the users having liked the product in freemium model, could sign up for subscription.

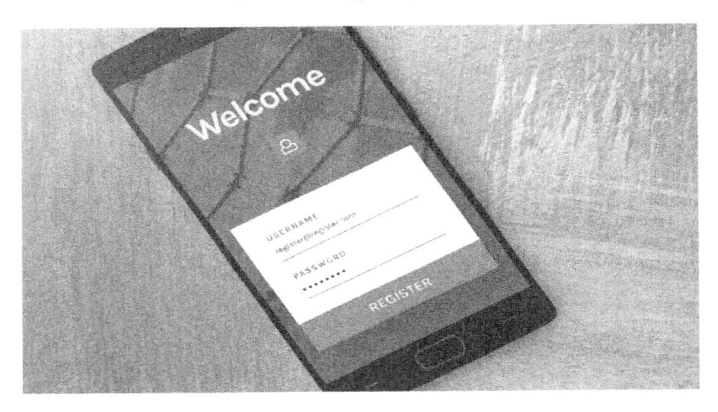

Make the customers realize how much they benefit if they become members. If you can get customers in the door with this plan, they will think of upgrading to a better plan if they like your product and services. While it is easy to get customers in the door, it can be expensive to support a large number of free customers.

A good strategy when it comes to pricing is to be upfront and transparent with your customers, avoid hidden fees. If customers find hidden fees and happen to see the competitors' prices reducing, they are likely to terminate the service with your company and subscribe to competitors. Putting it out there when it comes to your price is a strategy that can make potential customers feel as if your business is well established and successful.

A freemium model can be great to get people in the door, so to speak, but be cautioned. Set a time limit to those on a free subscription. It can get expensive to support a high level of non-paying customers. Netflix is a good example of this, they start you at a free trial and then require you to upgrade after 30 days. I would say that 30 days is on the higher side when it comes to trial period, rather limit it to 7 days.

An alternate way in this model is to offer service with some limitation in features to customers, with upgrade features for regular customers and members. These features allow the customer to experience the power of what you offer without all the features.

5) Promotional Model

How did it feel when you got a $0 delivery fee on your first Uber Eats order? Or did you get a cash amount of $10 for using the Uber app to take your first JUMP e-bike ride by a certain date? Did this cash amount get added to your Uber Cash balance, which you were able to use for Uber trips, JUMP bike and scooter rides, and Uber Eats orders? Or how did you feel when you got an email for taking 5 Uber rides for 50% of the actual charge in 2 weeks' time? I am sure you have come across one of the above-mentioned promotional announcements and felt good about it. This is the most popular strategy among many subscription businesses.

Give a free trial or provide the option to try a month of service for free. Promotional incentives can be a great method for convincing dissatisfied customers to stick around. For example, give 2 months free if they had an issue with your service or give a credit amount if there is an outage. When dissatisfied customers say no and leave, conduct surveys to know what they did not like in your product and services.

6) Pay as You Go Model

Have you rented a vehicle and gone on a trip in recent times? Yes, I am talking about the adoption of pay as you go model by car-share services. The newest generation of car-share services, which allow drivers to pay as they go instead of paying by the day, is now a viable option for both travelers in the US and those in select countries around the world. While these pay-as-you-go services were created with locals in mind, the industry's increasing presence in major US and European cities makes them an appealing option for out-of-town visitors. Instead of paying upfront, customers pay for what they use. It is practical to send an invoice to customers at the end of the month for the services they used instead of billing them upfront.

Pay-as-you-go pricing model can be beneficial for an organization since they are only required to pay for the actual volume of resources consumed rather than paying a flat rate for a bundle of services that they may not fully use.

It is a good idea to have a "pay as you go" plan when your end-users do not have a definite usage pattern and are not sure about committing for a specific period. The primary disadvantage to the client under this pricing model is the difficulty in predicting ongoing software expenses.

When end users are able to pay for these life-changing products in affordable increments, as opposed to only a pre-paid one-time amount, these products become accessible to low-income populations. Companies, therefore, can reach out to more customers, resulting in increased sales and revenue for their business.

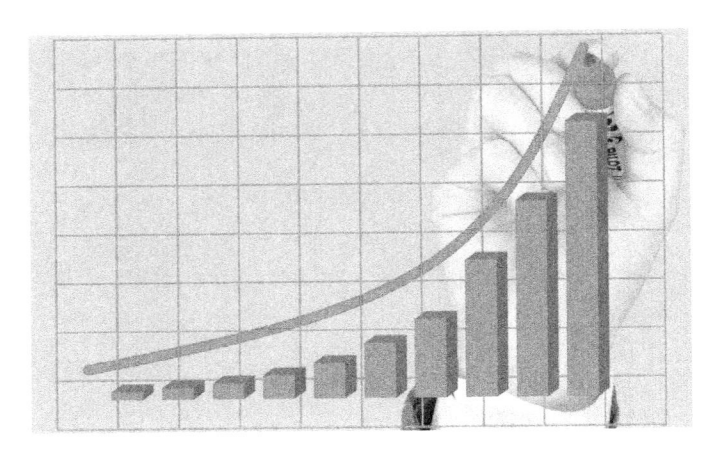

However, few companies are hesitant in choosing the pay as you go SaaS model as it is unpredictable for both customer and provider. Pay as you go excels when the unit of value is incremental and not monthly.

7) Overage Model

In this model, you set your price point upfront and charge the customers for extra usage. For example, take the case of calling a country outside US application where you get talk time of 100 minutes and are charged 10 dollars per month for it. Overage is like charging you, 1 dollar for every 5 minutes upon usage of 100 minutes. This model is being adopted rapidly across subscription businesses. There are various options to mix and match different strategies and create your own customized pricing for your subscription business.

You can always change the strategy if the model does not work.

To summarize, not every customer of yours will need the same plan, each one of them might have different goals and visions. They could have different numbers to achieve in business operations. Listen to what customers need and what they look forward to in your product and service. Group customers of similar interest and goals. You may design the pricing plan for customers of similar nature and interest and send out offers, discounts, promotions, and ads.

Chapter 5: KNOW YOUR CUSTOMERS

After going through this chapter, you will be able to understand how to enhance your relationship with the customers.

Customer Bonding

Do you remember going to an independent pharmacy on a consistent basis during your childhood where everyone working in the pharmacy knew your name? I remember my visits to independent pharmacies quite well as I felt welcomed over there. Can you still go to an independent pharmacy and get special treatment?

There have been some huge changes to pharmacies in certain nations, with some big chains looking to get into the prescription medicine business to create a one-stop-shop for customers. One-stop-shop is a place that offers a wide variety of products or services that customers need. In any case, the pattern demonstrates that the overall population still lean towards independent/freelance pharmacies over these big chains.

To start with, pharmacists knew their customers by name. The same cannot be said of big chain pharmacies. And customers who used an independent pharmacist were far more likely to say that the pharmacy went out of its way to fill prescriptions faster.

Customers who went to independent pharmacies were also more likely to report that the pharmacist suggested a lower-cost medicine. I have come across this scenario multiple times during my visits to the independent pharmacies. I used to check with the pharmacist if formula of the lower-cost medicine was same as the one I had initially asked them and buy the lower-cost medicine upon their confirmation. I do not think big chain pharmacies offer lower-price option for customers.

This is a good example of personalized customer service. Customer bonding helps transform new customers into raving fans. Personalized customer service builds loyalty and makes your company stand out.

This way, you will get repeat customers who might spend more than new customers. Loyal customers tend to tell the people around them about their good experience with a company, thus becoming ambassadors. You might wonder if independent pharmacies can compete against big chains in a fast-changing environment. With repeat and loyal customers, their adoption of subscription-based model should be easier.

Also, when pharmacies give their customers protection against any rise in medical bills, it will help to establish customer loyalty and also benefit the healthcare provider's business.

My uncle was in the agriculture business practicing monoculture, which is growing one crop at a time. His initial years were good, but his revenue dwindled over the years.

He thought about the widespread questions raised about the sustainability of the same crops that were grown every year. He switched to polyculture where different crops are grown in successive years. He told me that this switch solved a lot of pest problems too. He was able to revive his business. He then connected with customers more closely and allowed them to subscribe to harvests from his farms.

In return for subscribing to a harvest, customers received a monthly box of farm goods, which included in-season fruits, vegetables, and crops. He would meet the members, notify them of monthly updates, and invite them for harvest.

With digital technology, he can keep in touch with his customers electronically. This system is referred to as CSA – Community Supported Agriculture, and it is mostly used in the United States and Canada. Customers and stakeholders are involved to a great extent, resulting in a stronger consumer-producer relationship.

Customers may not always buy from your company, however, by maintaining good rapport, they will always be a good source of referrals. This will help in identifying the prospects, and moving them up the hierarchy to demo users, to customers, to loyal customers, to members. Programs such as customer satisfaction surveys, newsletters, videos, presentations and personalized communications will help in improving the relationship between you and the customers.

This raises a question. When do you think new customers will become hooked?

Take Netflix for example, story writers know how to engage viewers when they develop a main character and plot and end the episode in mystery, making viewers curious about what's going to happen in the next episode. Directors know how to reveal the story, they are adept at gradually revealing the surprise elements.

It is hard to engage viewers if the first couple of episodes in any series are not very good. The quicker the viewer gets engaged in the show, the more they will stay to the end.

The subscription model is just not about getting a project completed and then moving on to the next one, it allows the subscription-based company to develop a relationship with the customers and cater to their business needs as they change. A company has to offer various services, promotions, and discounts to customers. Subscription-based companies must follow a customer-first mindset.

Customer experience trumps product. When your customer is a member, she will speak for your product. There is not much difference between a customer and a member. A member is like a loyal customer or raving fan.

During my high school days, I used to eagerly wait for the next version of Sportstar Weekly. Sportstar is a fortnightly sports magazine published in India. It covers sports in India, including cricket, the unofficial national sport of India. Additional coverage of sports includes football, tennis and Formula One Grand Prix.

I would go to the store and buy it. But I had to reach the store on time as it used to go out of stock within no time. I signed up as a member to get the sportstar delivered to my home. This magazine was a big hit among sports fans and followers. The online version of Sportstar was launched three years ago. The portal, a one-stop destination for multiple sports, offers the Indian audience a platform to follow their favorite sports and sporting personalities.

This is where membership plays a significant role. In a subscription model, you can make 100 sales in a year and 100 new sales the following year. Also, you can add renewals. On the first day of the month, you'll know that a good percentage of last year's revenue is already booked due to renewals.

Let's say I have an Amazon membership and a membership with a tennis sports club. The kind of pride that is associated with both of them is entirely different. You can renew or terminate amazon subscription services anytime. As a member of a tennis sports club, I will be excited to take my friends and family to sports event on guest passes and get access to sports magazines.

Yes, I like having a membership with Amazon and enjoying her subscription services but the benefits the tennis sports club membership will provide are different. As relationships strengthen, customers will renew the services without much persuasion on your part.

Membership programs work better because customers would naturally have a strong emotional connection to your product and services. Remember that members or loyal customers are going to stick with your company no matter what. You as a company have to be ready to make the extra effort that will help you in conversion of customers into members. It doesn't take long to become a big business if you convert a few percent of customers into members month after month, year after year.

Chapter 6: CUSTOMER RETENTION STRATEGIES

After reading this chapter, you will have a better understanding of the following topics:

- Managing Customer's expectations
- Understanding customers' pulse and offering them irresistible offers
- Customer Focus
- Developing a Value proposition
- Reducing Customer churn and retaining customer subscriptions
- Believe in your product
- Charging for your content
- Advertise your product
- Early termination

Managing Customer's Expectations

Gone are the days when companies expected customers to keep coming back to them just because their product was good. To be honest, there isn't much difference between the companies in terms of the value that a product may offer. Price and product are important, but customer experience has started to outweigh them. Customer expectations are constantly changing and evolving from time to time. Customers do not switch companies solely because of cheaper prices that competitor companies offer but mainly because of poor service. This is where customer retention comes into the picture. Whether it is software or subscription, agriculture, or cosmetics, customers prefer to experience a product or service for a low monthly fee, rather than own it for a higher price.

As a result, more and more companies are looking to better understand the subscription business lifecycle and how they can ride the recurring revenue stream and stop customer churn. Customer retention refers to the ability of a company to retain customers. Customer retention is impacted by how many new customers are acquired, and how many existing customers churn by canceling their subscription, not returning to buy, or closing a contract.

Customer retention rate is calculated as below.

((# Customers at end of period - # Customers acquired during period)) / # Customers at start of period)) X 100

For example: Imagine you start the year with 30 customers, gain five new customers in the first quarter, and have one customer churn.

((34-5)/30)) X 100 = 96.66 % retention rate.

Retention helps you understand the effectiveness of your product, marketing, customer service, and pricing.

Once you know your rate, you should consider doing a survey of your churned customers to determine similarities in reasons for leaving or types of customers that leave.

Customer retention is important to any growing company because it measures not only how successful they are at acquiring new customers, but also how successful they are at satisfying existing customers. Retaining customers is also easier and more cost-effective than acquiring new ones. Returning customers spend more and buy more often and refer friends and family.

Your company's retention is not going to be static. I would recommend, you keep a constant check and calculate as well as optimize it. Direct your attention towards getting customers to stick around. Your role is to set a good business strategy and vision. Once this is clear, you can delegate technical aspects to experts the same way you trust your auditors to file your taxes. If you get the right strategy and tell your expectations to technical folks, they will handle.

Firstly, you need to focus on how to get your business strategy right. This will help in earning new revenue and achieving retention sooner, thus growing your business by leaps and bounds. Develop a plan to grow your business by upselling and rapidly expanding into new geographies, new products, and new areas.

Customer Focus

Every company should know that retaining customers is cost-effective than acquiring new customers. The investment required to acquire new customers is at least 4-5 times more than what's needed to retain existing customers. If you do not keep in touch with existing customers, their changing needs, you could be well losing them faster than you expect.

It is important to dedicate just as many resources to retain existing customers as you do to selling to new customers. And that's what your customer success team is for; to help customers see the value and achieve goals using your product or service. But there is more to it than just answering their phone calls and helping them onboard with your software. It is about creating a process from the very beginning that fosters communication, trust, and mutual growth.

A good retention strategy delivers the added benefit of word-of-mouth marketing. If your customers are happy with your product or service, they will become your advocates and tell others about you. This will help in branding your product to new areas, especially when they renew the subscription for next term. There is a level of validation that trumps just about everything you say when your customer prospects see others like them using the subscription product and succeeding with that.

When you have a subscription business, you need a method to collect the membership fees from your community. You could attempt to do this by sending out a manual invoice at the start of every billing period. This can be expensive and time-consuming.

Instead, you could use an auto-renewal system to collect payments automatically from your customers. There are several benefits for your business when using an auto-renewal payment scheme. For example, it reduces the amount of administration you and your team needs to do. There is a higher retention of customers for your business and you know exactly when payments are going to be made by your customers.

Understanding Customer's Pulse and Giving them Irresistible Offers

No matter how good your product or service is, the simple fact is that no one will buy it if they do not want it or believe they don't need it. And you can't persuade anyone that they want or need to buy what you are offering unless you clearly understand what it is your customers really want.

Customers' needs change from time to time, ask them about product-related annoyances they would like you to eliminate and how your products meet their expectations today, how you can meet their needs and help them achieve goals better, are there any other companies that meet their needs, what needs are consistently met, are there opportunities to meet the needs better, how do the products make them feel, what they like in your product, etc.

SATISFACTION
TRUST
ASSISTANCE
LOYALTY
SUPPORT
COMMUNICATION
FEEDBACK
SERVICE

Make sure to reach out to quite a few customers to get answers to the above questions. You may ask your customers using an online survey tool. Once you have gathered the survey responses and analyzed them, create a concise and powerful proposition. Focus on the conversion rate of customers to members or renewing customers. Having your customer's email address and contact number is a good start.

This should help customers of similar interest. There will be enthusiastic customers who will love your products. Make sure to let them know when you repackage the product and deliver an upgraded version. They may love it more and buy more from you. This will certainly help your business benefits to grow. Offering incentives and following up with cancelled customers can significantly increase your active subscriptions.

There are some customers who use your products or services only because other companies offer them at a higher price. Try to explain your product, how you can help solve their problems, make them understand what you can offer for them. You do not want a situation where a drop in your competitors' price makes you lose customers. These are some ways through which you can improve the conversion rate on customers.

When you are confident about the value your product can add to your customers, provide an irresistible offer to the customers, like cancel subscription anytime without cancellation fees. You may provide a cash back guarantee or a 110% refund if the products and services of your company fail to meet customer expectations.

A money-back guarantee works well with customers, this shows them you have confidence in your product. You can also give your customers irresistible offers in different ways.

Free trial without credit card

Have you heard of Chargebee? It is okay if you have not heard of it. Let me walk you through what it is. Chargebee is a subscription management system which helps you to handle recurring billing, invoicing, and trial management for your customers. They do not ask for credit card information when you sign up as a buyer. Chargebee only requests for an e-mail address and a phone number as part of the sign-up process. In this model, customers do not need a credit card to sign up with you. But it is up to you to have a dedicated sales rep team to follow up with the customers who availed the trial to get feedback about the product and know what can be done to serve their needs better.

Strike a balance during the trial period so that the customer gets to understand your product, it's benefits and value proposition. A clear understanding will help the customers take up the subscription services with you. Some users might be reluctant to give their credit card details to your company without knowing about your product and how it will help them. From a trust perspective, it might look like the end-end conversion rate might be higher when a company does not ask for your credit card versus when a company asks for a credit card. But I think a few or more users could create multiple IDs and keep using a free trial forever. One may think that free trials come up with limited features when compared to the premium/regular account. What if features available in the free trial alone served users' purpose? Why will they then sign up to be your customer? Also, you will not have an idea why trial users did not convert into customers. So, I will not recommend the free trial without credit card model.

Free Trial with Credit card

Have you ever signed up for a streaming service of ESPN sports channel, Willow TV, Hot Star, HBO subscriptions, or Amazon Prime? I wanted to give examples of free trials across fields hoping you would have subscribed to at least one of them so far. I have seen that most of the free trials come with a duration of 1 week. I am sure you kept track of the end date and would have given a thought if you wanted to continue the subscription or cancel it. This is way better than just advertising about your product and service with no free trial period.

Free trial with a credit card means that customers will be automatically upgraded to a payment plan after the trial period expires. Cancellation of the service has no fee when it is done before the trial period gets completed. If users would like to subscribe, all they have to do is not to cancel the subscription. You can add the feedback (survey) as a mandatory feature when users decide to cancel the subscription. Some of the users who would have used the free trial with serious intent might give a value feedback that will help you understand problems in your product and work on improving them.

By asking users to enter their credit card details, you are filtering users with serious intent and helping reduce the overhead follow-ups for your sales team. Users who liked the product will renew their subscription and become regular customers, and this will boost your trial to paid users number.

Free Trial, Credit card Extension

In this model, you provide free trial to customers without a need for a credit card. Once the free trial period is over, you may give the option to extend the trial period in exchange for a credit card number. This model yields good results. Most of the customers who have opted to extend the trial period have gone to become paid customers.

Extensions are better than losing a customer forever. Problems arise when you extend the trial and nothing else changes. So, it is important that you understand the reason behind the extension request. Get them to engage during the trial extension. Users may have genuinely needed that extension to understand the product better and decide if they want to take up the subscription or not. Also, your company may be offering 5 products in free trial and a 1-week trial period might not be enough for users to thoroughly evaluate and understand the products.

Promote Referral Programs

How did you feel when you got a cashback of $500 from a bank when a friend you referred signed up for a credit card and spent some amount? I am sure you felt good. Implement referral programs in your subscription-based companies as well. I have seen some companies limiting the referral programs for a short period. On fewer occasions, customers themselves don't know when referral programs are active. Do not limit the referral programs to existing customers alone. Sometimes, there might be colleagues or people in other departments or in their network who may find your product or service effective and might have the budget to spend.

You could plan a customer referral program with higher incentives for existing customers and lesser incentives for people who aren't already customers. You have got nothing to lose. This way, you will be taking care of existing customers in the right way and have a chance to expand your business by opening a referral program for non-customers.

When you ask your customers to recommend your product or service to friends and colleagues, you need to consider that they have spent their time and money to do the favor for you. If you reward them with the right incentives, they might be motivated to dedicate a bit more of their time to referring your product and service to friends and colleagues.

Many subscription-based companies make the mistake of only rewarding the referrer, but the success of your customer referral program depends on two sides. You need someone making the referral, and someone accepting the referral.

A successful referral is worth a lot to you, so it's important to offer your customer something valuable in return for their help. I have come across one or two successful referral programs and had the opportunity of being both the referrer and the person accepting the referral.

Develop an Easy Referral Process

Be it a new user sign up process or customer survey form, we all shy away from it when there are too many steps. Of course, we'll follow lengthy steps when we are in real need. Remember that the more time and effort it takes to send a referral, the less likely your customers are to do so. They are spending their time and effort for you, so it is important that you value that and come up with an easy procedure to complete the referral process. Therefore, the most important thing to remember when creating a customer referral program is to make the referral process quick and easy.

A good referral process should require no more than two steps to send the referral, and you should be able to make the referral in-app or on-page. A well-thought-out and well-written value proposition can help you grow your business too. Let's read more on what value proposition is and how it can help you grow your business.

Develop a Value Proposition

Some customers move out from the market and new customers come in the business. Make sure to reach out to customers who move away to know what needs you do not meet. A value proposition is a statement that clearly communicates who your target audience is, what needs they have, and how your products will meet those needs. What problems do you solve for them? Is there anyone who can solve the problems better?

On the off chance that you don't have answers to every one of these inquiries, it implies you need to develop your value proposition. There is not a single company that does not have web portal these days. You could place the shorter version of value proposition in the web portal so that it has a better chance of getting noticed by guest users and customers. Every business needs a reason for her customers to buy from them and not their competitors. This is called a Unique Sales Proposition (USP).

For example:

You could offer 5 per cent discount to customers that spend more than $200 a month - this would be a USP for cost-conscious customers.

It's a good idea to review your USPs regularly. Do a study of what customers like in your company – if it is product or service. Can you tailor your products or services to match your customers' needs? Consider asking your customers why they buy from you. Focus on finding the most enthusiastic customers, get to know their needs, what they look for in terms of betterment in your product and service.

Set up some time for discussion with your customers, hear their problems, let them know the best deal price and value you offer them through your product and services, understand their goals for the next one year, what numbers they want to achieve and propose them the solution to fix their problems.

Make sure to communicate your value proposition to your customers. At exactly that point will they acknowledge, understand and appreciate the value of your product and service. Poor communication is one of the predominant reasons for the poor conversion rate of customers into members. Make a point to embrace the right practice. Your company is guaranteed to grow in the long run irrespective of any negative trend in the industry if you do so.

Believe in your Product

Have you tried network marketing? I wanted to explore it, so I attended a few seminars where successful people had spoken about how to make it big in network marketing. Those seminars really motivated me, but before I could realize the true potential of network marketing, I lost faith and opted out, mainly because I was image-conscious.

Not going the traditional way is equivalent to going the wrong way where I grew up. Many people are too image-conscious and end up giving up on this wonderful industry. I too succumbed to it.

The success of any business principally depends on you believing in your product and service first. If you do, you will first attempt to promote and sell a product without much hesitation within your circle of family and friends.

You will then be able to extend it to colleagues, neighbors, and business associates. If you want to make it big, then you can promote it to strangers through offline advertisements like newspapers, pamphlet ads, etc. and online marketing like blogs, Facebook, WhatsApp, etc.

People now think of network marketing much more strategically than just a small part-time income source. But by the time people realize that direct selling involves some work, they lose faith.

I was talking to one of my college friends who recently joined network marketing. After reading about the subscription business model, I realized that success in network marketing is not just essentially multiplying the number of people in your network but also having members who buy your products and services regularly because they believe in you and your product.

I believed in a protein-rich product that my friend was selling as part of a business. I started buying the product once I believed it. The friend from whom I bought this product was doing well in the business. I shared my knowledge about the subscription model to my friend and recommended setting up a website portal where he could let customers register and enter their payment method and preferred term. Today he has 30 individuals (customers) buying products from him once a month. He gets recurring revenue without having to manually monitor how they are going. When I talked to him last time, he told me that his belief in the product keeps him going. His on-going announcements about the products and its new features via website portal has helped maintain good customer rapport. These on-going announcements have helped customers know about the products and its new features from time to time.

Many companies undermine their own product. They do not have an approach about how to promote or market their product. The truth is, successful companies do not keep inventing new products all the time but are excellent at repackaging it in accordance to the needs of customers. If your product is challenging to understand, make sure to offer free trials and demos as benefits.

On the off chance that you look profoundly, you will take care of similar troubles for customers at more than a few levels. The difference in the prices you charge your customers stems from the degree of service you're offering to them.

It is a good practice to ask your customers about how better you should explain your price proposition, what is the correct price, what would be the right trial period. Instead of debating among your groups on these parameters, it is nice to hear at once from customers. If you do no longer have the bandwidth to perform all this, rope in the right vendors and effectively communicate what you need from them, ask them to watch customers closely.

Advertise your Product

Most companies rely on social media platforms like Facebook, website users, and poll surveys to know about feedback for their product.

Advertising is a perfectly excellent revenue flow in this business. You have to suppose of how to brand your product and carrier to advertisers so that they can promote it to the proper customers. Branding is no longer a guarantee for accelerated sales. You can rent the first-class graphic designer, however if you put the greatest brand on an awful product, you won't go far. However, if you realize that your product is essentially the same as your competitor's, you might be able to gain the upper hand with better branding. What is inside the cup may be the same, but you can decorate the cup better.

For instance, Netflix does a good job in terms of promoting movies around global events like Christmas and Halloween. Once you watch a movie, other movies related to the one you just watched are displayed.

Reduce Customer Churn and Retain Customer Subscriptions

Churn is unavoidable for any subscription-based business. There are plenty of reasons why customers cancel (or) terminate their subscription. Customers optout sometimes because they know current plan lacks the value they expect, and they do not have the budget to opt for a better plan which will get them better value. Too frequent as well as too little communication from you can trigger the customers to cancel (or) terminate the subscription. What you must do is to identify the churn coming from avoidable sources, and work to minimize unnecessary cancellations. Try to make sure that your messages are always valuable and important and conveyed at right intervals. As a company, you can try to draw them back with an offer of upgrade.

I am sure you have faced this scenario while cancelling cable service plan or internet service. One very common source of churn is expired payment information. Customers need to make sure that they keep a track of their credit cards' expiry date and update the payment information on time.

In a subscription-based model, cloud customers typically pay upfront, prior to receiving access to cloud services. Prices are often based on the subscription's term period and a longer subscription often translates to a lower cost. In a subscription-based model, cloud customers commonly pay forthright, before getting access to cloud services. Costs are frequently founded on the subscription's term period and a longer subscription regularly means a lower cost. For subscription businesses, the longer customers are with you, the happier they should become.

The key to retention is what you do after new customers subscribe. Effectively and correctly handling new customers can greatly increase your customer lifetime value. This can provide a lot of stability to your business. You will be able to invest more to get new customers with a strong base. This will give you an edge over your competitors. With more customers, you get more referrals and you can attract more investors who might show interest in your business.

To get new customers to the retention point, you need to build good relationships. The retention point is the moment when your customers fully believe in your product and services. Your company has to scale up and operate in the right way as there are too many competitors out there in the market. You are competing with the best attention seekers in the market. Getting your new customers to the retention point quicker is the secret to cutting down churn rate.

New customers will have to decide if they want to be part of your group at the retention point. You can inspire new customers to the retention point by letting them know the benefits they'll get from using your products and services. At this stage, you shouldn't talk about pitfalls. Talking about pitfalls can cause doubts in new customers. Spend time on developing promotional videos about your product and services. Make sure you keep it short. A 1-minute video will be received better than a 3-minute video. It could be surprisingly easier to convert new customers to long term customers when you work on moving them to the retention point.

Create a customer focused team tasked with examining and refining the entire customer acquisition process lifecycle. Ask account managers to identify customers who aren't using the software frequently and work with them to identify their goals and needs. The customer focus team should look at common customer issues such as product features, the user interface, and support materials.

Customers are far more likely to cancel their subscription than contact your company to complain. A good practice is to identify customers who have stopped using your subscription services (or) product and send e-mails encouraging them to tell you about their issues and offering to help get them back on track.

You may want to remind customers of the value proposition your product delivers. Use e-mail marketing, social media, your website, and other client touchpoints to re-iterate the value of using your software.

Be ready to go the extra mile to help your customers solve a problem until they are satisfied with the solution. Make sure to follow up on their service requests and problems, this will make them feel important. Also, find out if things are going well and if there is any further assistance you can offer.

When a customer uses your solution to achieve a milestone in her business, you may send her a congratulatory email and ask if she needs any help in improving any feature in the future. If your product already has upgraded features that are ready to be rolled out, ask your customers if they want to learn more about it. Plan a demo for the customers and get their feedback. You will know exactly what customers like in your product.

Additionally, you could offer any of the various content below you believe will be helpful for your customers:

- Videos
- Blog posts
- eBooks
- Webinars
- Customer forums
- Customer success stories
- FAQs
- Best practices in the industry

Happy customers share their experiences with friends and colleagues. Go out of your way to foster happiness and goodwill with unsolicited expressions of your appreciation.

As part of your renewal process, you may send an e-mail to thank your customers and consider taking your appreciation a step further with small gifts or bonus offers.

Follow this one simple rule to design an onboarding flow that works. Your customers should never be left in a confused state about what to do next, or why. Make sure to educate your customers about the product and its benefits. Let them know how you could help customers' business grow, if they have one. If customers happen to be the end users with no business to grow, it will then just be a demo on the products for them. Try to reduce customers' effort and make them feel cared for. Also, you could automatically upgrade your customers' account. This could be the ultimate customer appreciation gift. It can go a long way in winning customers' loyalty.

Imagine your customer suddenly receiving an email or call to learn you have bumped their plan to a higher level with more powerful features. Doing so may cost you nothing, produce good results in the retention process, and create enthusiastic brand advocates.

Charging for your Content

I have noticed that many publishers are afraid to charge users for access to their content. This is a big mental roadblock if you think no one will pay for your content. This fear comes from the fact that competitors give away a lot of content for free. So, when you charge for the same content you feel insecure. When you are in business, you need to believe in yourself that your content is better than your competitors'.

Giving away some of your content is essential for driving awareness about your product and interest in your membership. Different content could serve different purposes and target different customers. You need to choose what is ideal to give away for nothing. A few organizations come up short since they are bad at making sense of what ought to be free, what ought to be paid, and who is eager to pay among their customer base.

You need to figure out how to ensure your content isn't accessible by all. Paywall is a game plan whereby access is confined to customers who have paid to buy in to the site. You can't anticipate that individuals should begin paying for your content when paywall is set up. There should be a procedure around setting up a paywall. This is the place subscription model scores. You charge your customers for utilization of content over a given period, after this period they can end or restore the services.

Many companies do not know how to shift to making money by charging for their content. To avoid making mistakes while selling content, you need to develop a good understanding of who your customers are, their business, and what they want to achieve.

Early Termination

You might wonder how early termination topic fits in customer retention strategies section. You will know the answer shortly. Early termination is cancellation of subscription by customer before the end of her initial term. This could be because they no longer need the product, they are not satisfied with the product.

An early termination fee is the charge levied when a party wants to break the term of an agreement or a long-term contract. Termination fees are common to service industries such as cellular telephone service, subscription television, etc.

For instance, a customer who purchases cellular phone service might sign a 2-year contract which is inclusive of $400 fee when the customer breaks the contract. This was initially viewed as a strategy to survive in the market. Some of the customers even complained about this contract as they could not migrate to superior services with ease. I have experienced scenarios where I wanted to downgrade from the premium package in my cable services to the normal package plus internet services because the charge was increasing from the current term to the next term.

There was a live agent, probably a retention specialist, who negotiated with me and offered same services at a lesser price or upgraded services at a price lesser than what was advertised on their website.

These agents must be receiving commissions based on how many accounts they keep active. So, I would recommend using it to your advantage and trying something like, "This service is too expensive, I will renew or upgrade my services if it were cheaper" and see what happens.

Checking with your company which offers the products and services is very important, especially if your reason for canceling is due to, for example, not getting access to all the special channels in a streaming service. A customer retention agent may offer you a package upgrade or premium channels for no extra charge. Make sure to ask how long these offers are valid to avoid more surprise fees in the future.

Retention agents might give free streaming or credits to keep your business. Ask them clearly how long the current charge would hold and connect again on time. I know this is a tip I am providing to the user community while I have suggested most of the tips in this book to companies on how to manage subscription business effectively. All of us are end users for some one's business. Isn't it?

Have you ever given thought about letting your subscription expire rather than paying cancellation fees when you break the contract? If not, give it a thought as early termination fees could cost you more.

Let's say for instance you have a contract with a Cable provider and want to discontinue the service before the end of the contract period. You don't want to end your service if your cancellation fee is higher than what it would cost you to pay out the duration of your subscription. So, one good strategy is to wait until your contract expires. Having said that, you need to remember the term end date to avoid automatic renewal in this case.

Chapter 7: REWARD YOUR CUSTOMERS

After reading this chapter, you will be able to understand about customer reward programs better.

Reward Programs

I am sure you've used the Uber app for booking car rides to commute locally. And if you have regularly used the Uber app, you would have got a notification that the next 5 rides come with 50% off for each of your next 5 rides (up to $10 per ride) this month. Or, have you ever got a notification for being in the top 10% of highest-rated riders from Uber? This recognition of Uber to you for being a great member of the Uber community must give you a good feeling about your conduct during Uber rides.

A new user does not get this notification from Uber. How did it feel when you got this notification from Uber? Regular customers/members would have really liked that and perhaps used the Uber app more. This is one way to reward your loyal or regular customers. The customers/members feel special when they get a reward or incentive. In the competitive subscription market, your business needs every advantage it can possibly use to get ahead. Introducing rewards and loyalty schemes will help to grow your customer base and retain the old customers as well.

In the subscription model, you could reward customers with a 20% discount on a specific product, a configuration (or) offer 24*7 support for one of the products ordered by the customers for a specific time period. In the competitive market, your business needs every advantage it can possibly use to get ahead. Introducing rewards and loyalty schemes will help to grow your customer base and retain the old customers as well.

Many successful subscription-based companies are turning to loyalty and rewards programs throughout different stages of the customer retention lifecycle. How do you decide what is right for your program?

SaaS will have positive results outside of incentivizing current customers to refer others, and rewards for loyalty to your SaaS can have good results. The primary motive behind a loyalty program is to retain customers by rewarding them for their repeat purchase behavior. The main thing you need to know is that not all loyalty schemes are effective. You have to customize the basic loyalty programs and adapt it to get better results.

For a subscription-based customer, a loyalty program is not going to be quite the same as getting a double star on every single order at Starbucks coffee. You need to think what makes those bonus stars special? It is simple. The reward is meaningful as it is something that the customer already likes and can use.

In the subscription model, you could choose to reward loyalty over time, for example, offering additional features, a free month, discounted pricing or other rewards that aligns with the type of people who use your product for every year forward.

You could talk to your members and find out what they would like as an additional feature. The idea is that by offering them something closely related to the product, the reward becomes useful to them. Make the rewards attainable.

You would have heard of the airline miles program where the awards are so elusive, or so based in conditions for what you can redeem them for that they are not really worth going for. This kind of reward will not interest all your customers. A few of them may get frustrated and give up. Loyalty and rewards schemes are much more effective if awards are achievable in a simple manner and easy to cash in. If you set too many complicated rules around your program, you might as well not bother.

Have you ever thought of having different tiers of subscription like how airlines have classes? You could tie in your rewards to different tiers of subscription. This could encourage more purchases and memberships.

Amazon Prime is a good example of how offering something extra to a more elite tier can encourage purchases. Members receive benefits, which include free fast shipping for eligible purchases, streaming of movies, TV shows and music, shopping deals and selection, unlimited reading, and more. While they are estimated to make a significant loss on their free two-day shipping offer for Prime members, they make up for it by the significant increase in spending of Prime members over non-members.

I would recommend you set goals, monitor them at regular intervals to understand how successful the loyalty and rewards program has been. Try to remain relevant to the customer and make sure your loyalty scheme provides them with some incentive. If you're not sure, send out a survey to your customers and ask if the loyalty program is a motivator for them.

Reward your members and customers for the referrals they provide. Know your referral stats first. Before you implement any new rewards or referral program, your best course of action is to understand your current referral data. How many of your customers came to you because some other existing customer referred them? You should develop the capability to find this out through analytics.

It is important to know your current referral stats first because you want a baseline for any program you put in place. It is worth knowing about how many subscription-based customers came in due to referrals. You could create a un-complicated loyalty program that delivers rewards with discounts, value-added bonuses, or special members-only content.

You could inspire your customers to use your software more often or vigorously by adding a fun element to the experience. Conduct a goal-based fun event or a competition and recognize the progress towards the goal.

Upselling your service is a good strategy. Some of them view it as an opportunity to achieve the retention soon. There could be some customers who will benefit immensely from your solution. So, upselling is definitely a good idea. You will be able to make more profit and also win an even more loyal client.

You could offer support to your customer along with the subscription.

Category	Standard	Premium
Hours of coverage	Standard business hours	24* 7 support for severity 1 and 2
Support coverage	Phone	Web and Phone
Number of cases	Unlimited	Unlimited

Take an active Red Hat subscription, for example. This subscription provides everything needed to run your mission-critical systems securely. As part of the subscription, customer gets access to a community of experts, knowledge resources, security updates, and support tools.

Ongoing delivery - Patches, bug fixes, updates, upgrades

Technical support - 24/7 availability, unlimited incidents, routing, multi-vendor case ownership

- Commitments – Certifications, software assurance
- Expertise - Security Response Team (SRT), Customer Portal, Knowledge base

At any point in time, someone must be approaching your current customers and offering them more value in terms of features, service, and price. See if you can increase the value of your service by upgrading it for your customer.

Delight your current customers by adding more benefits and perpetually fulfilling their hunger for additional. Attempt to release new forms that offer more benefits, and services to customers, and don't hike your charges when you do. Make your customers mindful of what is in store in the next upgrade and how it will benefit them.

Connect with customers via social media to improve the relationship. Follow your customers and interact when appropriate. Utilize online networking to understand your customers. Keep a tab on industry improvements. Make your customers special. Be accessible to respond to every single open inquiry from your customers. In the event that your organization has facilitated a site, consider having a BOT to manage a customer through fundamental inquiries. Brisk and concerned reactions to any grievances or issues will go far toward winning customer's trust and confidence.

Conduct exit interviews for your outgoing customers. Hear them out about what they did not like in your product, and what they expected and did not get. You cannot acquire two customers and lose one customer before the renewal of services in the next term. This will impact the growth of the business. There ought to be an exercise gained from losing a customer.

Associate with those customers who want to cancel (or) terminate their subscriptions or the customers who have thought of doing the same. I see a few customers won't discuss why they are leaving you. When dissatisfied customers say no and leave, conduct surveys to know what they did not like in your product and services. Track your endeavors to retain their subscription. Do what you can to learn more about their successes and failures with your solution. What you learn may prove invaluable for creating more value for existing customers, improving retention and further refining your retention strategies and practices.

Chapter 8: SUBSCRIPTION RENEWALS

After reading this chapter, you will be able to understand the following topics better:

- Auto-renewal subscriptions
- Effective ways to handle subscription renewal
- Manual renewal subscriptions

"We want you back! Renew today for a 10% discount."

Have you ever received a message like the one above? Monitoring customer churn rate is a basic requirement for any subscription-based business. Renewal oriented promotions are well worth the effort.

Your renewal rate is a key metric which indicates both the current level of customer loyalty as well as the overall quality of your product or service. Auto-renewal subscriptions and manual renewal subscriptions are the two types of renewal subscriptions in place.

Auto-Renewal Subscriptions

Auto-renewal subscription is a subscription that will get renewed before your current subscription term expires.

With auto-renewal, you will never miss an issue of your favorite magazine. You always receive the lowest renewal price for your subscription term. You can avoid multiple renewal notices and telemarketing calls. Payment details are already available on the file, so no time is wasted in reaching out to the customer for an invoice.

Auto-renewal duration can be for a month or 12 months. Before you are automatically billed for your next term, you should be notified of the rate of your renewal, and you can then change your credit card, address information, or cancel before the order is placed.

Typical examples of this renewal type are monthly cable TV bills, annual anti-virus definitions, and per-gigabyte data storage fees. Because customers are familiar with what the billing amount will be, they are typically okay with automatic payment.

Auto-renewal is one of the most popular methods for subscription businesses to sign up customers. While they have significant benefits for the business, customers are sometimes unaware of the advantages they gain from signing up to an auto-renewal system; advantages such as no service interruption, easy and automatic payment process, and subscription cancellation.

Convenience for Your Customers

I have noticed that many customers hesitate to enter into a contract where they are re-billed at a pre-defined schedule. Rather than forcing the subscriptions to be taken up, make your customers understand that there are types of renewals – manual renewal and auto-renewal.

This allows you to save costs in manually sending and processing invoices. You could then invest the funds elsewhere in the business or offer your customers a more competitive price.

The major benefit for your customers is the convenience an auto-renewal subscription model offers. This will enable customers to plan and do better finance management. Also, a few companies offer discounts when auto-renewals are done.

Simplified Cancellation Process

One of the major concerns that customers have is the time taken to cancel a subscription. Some customers feel like they have to go through a lengthy cancellation process, in terms of talking to a customer representative and submitting the cancellation request with the reason for cancellation. The customer may just want some email updates right from the moment the cancellation was submitted to complete the cancellation process.

This should be possible from the company's banking dashboard. This means the payments can be stopped immediately, instead of waiting for your company's administration team to process the cancellation.

At the same time, your company's online system can be updated, and access restricted immediately. Likewise, the distribution team can be informed of the cancelled subscriptions and remove the customers from the mailing list. Product or/and service dissatisfaction is not the only reason why customers cancel or terminate their subscription. We discussed in one of the earlier chapters about some of the valid reasons why customers cancel or terminate a subscription.

Having a complicated cancellation procedure is going to further drive away the customers from your company. It is unlikely that they will come back to you again. You should make the cancellation process very simple for your customers.

Manual Renewal Subscriptions

The customer is not billed for the next term period until the customer willingly agrees to renew, and that will allow the company to charge her.

The customer may change their credit card information before the next term period starts. A good example of this type of subscription is a utility bill or Comcast internet bill. You subscribe to electricity and natural gas, but you generally choose to complete payment manually each month because you want to see and approve the amount before paying the bill.

Customers are familiar with subscriptions that have automatic billing but are also more likely to complain if they are upset with the way that companies go about implementing automatic subscription renewals.

Here are some benefits of automatic subscription renewal process.

- Service continues until the customer cancels it
- No manual intervention is required by the marketing team to convince the customer to renew the services
- Auto-renewal, as the name suggests, provides higher renewal rates. This is when customers become members and develop a strong belief in your product and service
- Incremental cost is minimized because the product was already delivered successfully

For all these reasons, companies love an automatic recurring subscription. The typical renewal rate for a monthly automatic subscription is in the 90+

percent range. For annual cycles, the number drops into the 80s because of expiring credit cards and accounts.

However, as automatic recurring subscriptions apply to online products, there are quite a few drawbacks that companies need to consider.

- Increased refunds and chargebacks because of customer forgetfulness and marketing tactics
- Increased customer contacts to support inquiry about credit card charge or account debit
- Offline payment methods, like wire transfers, require customer action, so you need to send reminders to them via e-mail

Before deciding for or against the automatic renewal process, consider the pros and cons of manual subscription renewal. The pros of manual subscription renewal are as follows:

- Low level of customer complaints, refunds, and chargebacks because of an advanced renewal notice
- Ability to increase renewal rates by optimizing your marketing message
- Additional marketing opportunities while communicating about the original purchase billing cycle

- Receive real market feedback concerning product pricing/positioning by testing renewal efforts
- Modify renewal price when re-marketing to customers to increase the renewal rates

However, some cons need consideration as well:

- Renewal rates are lesser in manual renewal process when compared to auto-renewal process
- Requires a lot of manual efforts to send renewal marketing messages, follow through
- Requires a new purchase order for each subsequent billing event

For example, you can recommend your customers to set up the payment mode as manual if they do not prefer billing amount being deducted automatically. This way, customers will be able to check the invoices and make the payment manually.

This applies to many subscription products. However, if the time frame is longer, like six months or a year, then manual renewal may be best to reduce the complaints about automatic charges. This can apply to anti-virus and anti-malware software products.

Effective Ways to Handle Subscription Renewal

Once you have your baseline metrics on customer renewal rates, move on to develop and implement a strategy to improve renewals. Part of that strategy must be to make it easy for your customers to renew their subscriptions. Below are a few effective ways to handle subscription renewal.

Tailor your offer to what Customers need with Flexible Pricing

Make your products customizable so that customers can choose and pay for only the features they want. Pricing may also differ based on the size of the organization. For example, users at a startup might not be willing or ready to pay abundant money for an accounting software however they most likely don't have the same needs as enterprise users, so it makes sense for them to pay less for an efficient version of your product.

Offer Automatic Renewals

Set automatic renewals from the start or provide special offers for changing from manual to automatic. The best way to convince customers to switch renewal types is by setting up migration campaigns and running promotions. Of course, you could also offer manual renewal discounts, but keep in mind that, statistically, automatic renewal rate is typically four times higher than manual renewal rate.

Notify Customers when it is time for renewal

If automatic renewals are enabled against the original subscription order, always let customers know when their credit card is going to be billed, a little bit before the end of the current term period.

If customers have manual renewal enabled, you can attract them with discounts for early renewals. Make sure to follow up with customers in this period, remind them about the benefits of using your product and service and wait for their decision. Do not send too many emails because you do not want to annoy them. If customers do not opt for manual renewal and the subscription expires, you can still try to get the customers back with a discount.

Offer Multiple Renewal Methods

To keep your customers, you have got to provide them the flexibility to decide on however they need to renew their subscriptions. They could renew the service automatically or manually renew through self-service, customer support, or per the business process designed for it. You just have to make all the options clear and help customers choose the most convenient renewal method for them.

Reach out to your customers concerning their renewal choices through in-product electronic messaging, or period messages concerning subscription expiration. Also, certify you usually permit customers to purchase renewals in their native currency.

Offer Grace Periods

If your customers forget to renew, don't simply stop their access to your product or service. Offer them a grace period and add a few additional days to their subscription. This way, they get the prospect to settle on whether or not they need to renew or not and act in like manner. Customers appreciate having access, even with a past-due subscription because it gives them time to update their payment details and back up their data.

Use Tools to proactively avoid Passive Churn

I have heard that the Account Updater Service is a tool that ensures billing continuity for active subscriptions, significantly increasing your renewal and authorization rates. It allows you or your supplier to automatically update credit card data for customers when cardholder data changes.

Make the Renewal Process simple

A complicated renewal process might drive away customers. Make sure to set up a procedure to connect with customers to realize their choice on renewing the service for the following term time period. The significant thing is telling customers that they can contact you whenever to get some information about renewals. When the current term period, say a 12-month subscription, is coming to an end, what would you do to make customers renew?

When the current term period is coming to an end, and you are about to enter a new term period (duration – 12 months), if you are not sure about billing your customers without asking permission from them, it means your relationship with the customer is not great. That means you don't know if your customers are successful with your product or what product and which features, they like the most.

If you had a decent relationship along with your customers, you wouldn't be scared of telling them that you just are progressing to bill them for future term amount. If you're unsure however customers would react, and if charge is completed without their notice as a result of their credit card was on the payment setup, you'll be troubled that your customers would possibly ask for a refund next. Asking customers for forgiveness when charging them for services is probably going to cause mass cancellations or chargebacks.

If you are only interacting with your customers once a year, you are probably not heavily focused on customer success, their goals, or their changing business needs.

You do not really know who is likely to churn and who is a good candidate for renewal. You are not engaged with the customer at all when you stay in contact with them just to tell them that you have charged them for the following term time frame; you're not connecting with them to understand their feedback about your product; you haven't asked if there is a scope of improvement in product features or what their objective is.

Whichever way you choose to go, carefully consider the buying behavior of your customers. As the behaviour of online shoppers evolve, you may find even more opportunities in automatic or manual subscription billing.

Chapter 9: MEASURING THE PERFORMANCE OF YOUR SUBSCRIPTION BUSINESS

After reading this chapter, you will be able to understand how to measure the performance of your subscription-based business. Measuring the performance of your company is a necessary step in progressing in the right direction. Isn't it? If you need to improve business (or) simply build upon current success, it is a process that can greatly impact operations. Recurring revenue is the main positive factor of any subscription-based business. Most SaaS businesses work on a monthly subscription model and it is very appealing. Customers get to pay a fixed fee, each month. The company can be sure to have predictable revenue if your customers stay with you.

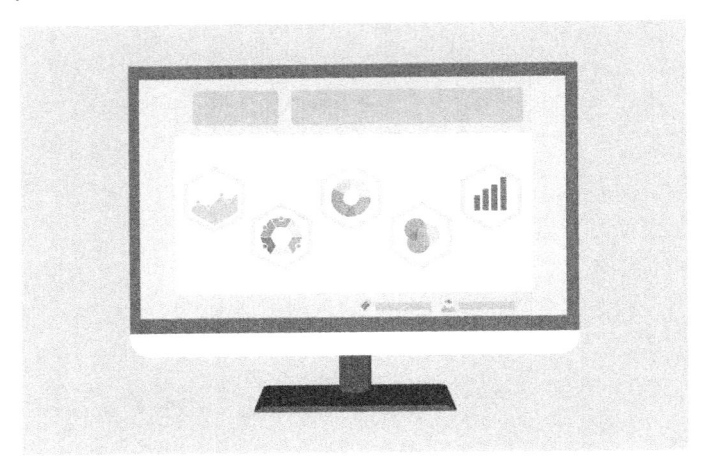

Monthly Recurring Revenue, referred as MRR, is probably the most important metric at all of any subscription-based business. You don't have to worry about one-off sales every month once you acquire a new customer you got a recurring revenue. Having said that, factors like retention and churn pose a challenge.

Let's say you have two customers A and B for your company. Customer A pays $100 per month and Customer B pays $200 per month. Your company's MRR would be $100 + $200 = $300.

To analyze MRR and specially MRR growth, you should consider three different aspects of MRR.

MRR Parameters

New MRR

New MRR is the new revenue brought by brand new customers acquired. So, let's say you have acquired on a given month 4 new customers paying $100 per month and 2 new customers $200 per month. Your New MRR for that month would be $800.

Expansion MRR

When customers upgrade their plans or buy additional products or services, revenue expands. This is a change modify – add scenario. That is when expansion MRR comes into the picture. So, let's say you have 3 customers that upgrade their plans from $100 per month to $200 per month. Your Expansion MRR for that month would be $300.

Churn MRR

Churn MRR is the revenue that has been lost from customers canceling or terminating or downgrading their plans. So, let's say on a given month you had 2 cancellations of $200 per month plans and other 2 customers downgraded their plans from $200 per month to $100 per month. You Churn MRR would be $600 [(2* 200) + (1* 100) + (1* 100)]. This means recurring revenue will be $600 lesser from next month onwards unless any other change is done in the current month. I recommend your company to monitor Churn MRR trend on a regular basis as it's a key metric. Higher Churn MRR calls for optimization and improvement in your product.

MRR Growth

You have learned about new MRR, expansion MRR and churn MRR. So, what is the overall MRR growth?

Below is the formula to calculate net new MRR.

Net New MRR = New MRR + Expansion MRR – Churn MRR

In the example below, you as a company have a monthly subscription cost of $300, and 2 customers in January. In February, you gain another customer, and MRR increases as a result.

January: 300 + 300 = $600 MRR

February: 300 + 300 + 300 = $900 MRR

March: 300 + 300 + 300 = $900 MRR

With below example, you will be able to learn about MRR and IMRR (Incremental MRR). Say, a customer has an active subscription for $500 in January month. Since this is a new order, MRR is equal to IMRR. This customer opts for upselling of $500 in February month. So, IMRR would be +$500. MRR will can be calculated as $500 + $500 = $1000. In the month of March, same customer opts for down sell of $250, IMRR = -$250. MRR can be calculated as $1000 - $250 = $750.

In the month of April month, the same customer opts for termination/cancellation of subscription, IMRR = -$750.

MRR can be calculated as $750-$750 = 0.

Month	January	February	March	April
MRR	$500	$1,000	$750	0
IMRR	$500	+$500	($250)	($750)
Comments	Subscription starts. If ORDER TYPE = NEW, then IMRR = MRR	Incremental revenue	Decremental revenue	Cancellation/ Termination

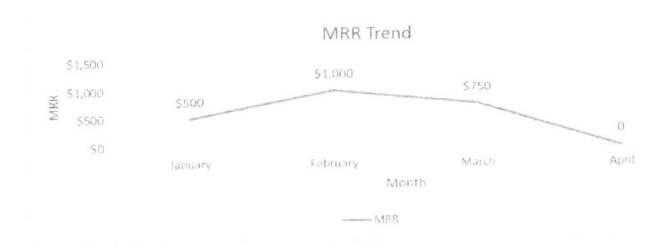

MRR Trend chart: January $500, February $1,000, March $750, April 0

If you want the recurring revenue to be calculated for the annual period, we get annual recurring revenue (ARR).

ARR = MRR*12

For forecasting purposes, ARR is used to predict annual recurring revenue for the coming 12 months, assuming no changes to your customer base. It is pretty straight forward, isn't it? There are a few things that you need to consider during the calculation of MRR. They are as follows.

- Monthly subscription fees, and any additional recurring charges for extra users, services
- Upgrades and downgrades
- Churn revenue
- Discounts

If your customer is on a $200 per month package, but pays a discounted monthly fee of $150, their MRR contribution is $150, not $200

MRR is not a true indicator of profitability but just revenue. We are trying to gauge trends in recurring revenue generation and adding costs to this will only confuse matters.

MRR is relatively easy to calculate if all your revenue comes from monthly subscriptions. But what happens if your customers want to pay for a year in advance?

In the example below, your company has 3 customers, and a monthly charge of $200. While 2 of the customers pay monthly, the third pays for the whole year in advance.

If you treat the advance as MRR, your monthly reporting might look something like this.

January: 200 + 200 + 2400 = $2800 MRR

February: 200 + 200 + 0 = $400 MRR

March: 200 + 200 + 0 = $400 MRR

Annual payment done by customer cannot be counted as MRR as it is onetime payment and not recurring one. Booking amount would be the total value of all new deals obtained over a time period, with no distinction between up-front and recurring payments.

Your bookings figure is great for calculating cashflow, but MRR is a measure of recurring revenue generation. So, to turn a booking into MRR, it needs to be amortized and spread out over the year. This way, you will be reporting the right booking amount.

January: 200 + 200 + (2400/12) = $600 MRR

February: 200 + 200 + (2400/12) = $600 MRR

March: 200 + 200 + (2400/12) = $600 MRR

Let's say, December is the year-end closure month in your company. Your company has 3 customers, and a monthly charge of $200. While 2 of the customers pay monthly, the third pays for the whole year in advance. Reporting 200 + 200 + 2400 as the booking amount for December may make your management happy but it isn't the right way to report. It is right to report 200 + 200 + (2400/12) as the booking amount for December.

Chapter 10: SUCCESS STORIES

The subscription business model continues to grow in popularity and is here to stay. It is one of the predominant business models for modern software. It is hard to find an industry that has not seen at least one subscription success story in the last few years. Let us go through few success stories in below section.

Amazon Prime Subscription

Amazon Prime is a subscription service that gives members access to a variety of perks. Their service has expanded into many other areas, including offering free streaming movies and music, rapid delivery options, and discounts on groceries. Some of the key contributions that Amazon Prime gives to customers are recorded underneath.

• Allows access to Amazon Prime Video, free 2-day sending on Amazon buys, access to selective arrangements on Amazon Prime Day, and an assortment of other Amazon-specific services

• Offers prime individuals an additional 10 percent off things available to be purchased at Whole Foods Markets just as extra value cuts every week on select items

• Allows moment access to a huge number of films and TV appears, including Amazon original series

• Allows access to in excess of 800,000 digital book titles and lets customers to get one every month, with no due date

• 20 percent off diapers through the site's Subscribe and Save administration and 15 percent off qualified items from your child vault

• Offers free 2-hour conveyance of food supplies and an increasingly restricted arrangement of items in select urban areas

• Allows you to have bundles conveyed to choose vehicles to help forestall bundle burglary

• 5 percent back on buys made at amazon.com and entire nourishment through amazon prime rewards signature card

Your company's success relies on your customers. The best approach for achieving good customer satisfaction levels is to develop a customer focused culture. A majority of amazon prime members visit the amazon website at least once a week. For exercises like perusing for new arrangements and limits, looking at costs, and checking accessibility, Amazon is really the 'one-stop search' for buyers. Concentrating on what customers need has driven a significant number of Amazon's most gainful business moves. Amazon's customer driven model gives motivation which any business could profit and take in an exercise from.

For additional details on Amazon prime subscription, please visit the below link.

https://www.amazon.com/amazon-prime-subscription/s?k=amazon+prime+subscription

Dollar Shave Club

I am sure you know about Dollar Shave Club, an American company based in Venice, California, that delivers razors and other personal grooming products to customers by mail. Dollar Shave Club team has executed incredibly well on many dimensions. They have built a brand that people love, that speaks authentically, and connects at an emotional level. They have worked very hard to launch new products, improve margins, spend money effectively on advertising, and many more strategies.

For a long time, Gillette has overwhelmed the dispensable razor game. To start with, the Dollar Shave Club originators nailed the two significant agony purposes of purchasing razors.

- The in-store razor purchasing knowledge is terrible

- Razors are getting costly. Getting razors on your doorstep when you need them is more helpful than heading to a store

Dollar Shave Club delivers razor blades on a monthly basis and offers additional grooming products for home delivery. They have made quality razors and blades much more affordable for customers. They created the web expertise of shopping for in to razors each basic and fun.

The membership service first launched on March 6, 2012, via a YouTube video that went viral. The YouTube video pulled in an unforeseen measure of traffic, that smashed the organization's server in the primary hour. When the server was re-established, Dollar Shave Club group satisfied the 12,000 requests that landed in the initial 48 hours of propelling the video.

A good launch will create an invaluable amount of momentum for your business. That is what Dollar Shave Club did.

Subscription is one key element to the business that has made it so successful. What many individuals could have over-looked concerning the ability of the dollar Shave Club is that the power of subscription.

People buy razors, need to change the blades frequently, and the majority shave on a really regular basis. This is a product category that advances itself perfectly to subscription on a long-term basis. They had paid close attention to why subscribers churn and have worked hard to address these issues and improve that retention. To change business of high churn rates into an effective one demonstrates the measure of planning they have done.

It has helped them edge over their competitors. Above all, Dollar Shave Club has created an amazing customer experience, and that has manifested itself in a subscription service that retains its users at high levels. Dollar Shave Club has demonstrated anybody can take on the huge folks and win.

For additional details on this topic, please visit the below link.

https://www.dollarshaveclub.com/get-started/how-it-works

Cisco's Focus on Subscriptions

Cisco has been consistently shifting their focus towards recurring software and subscriptions. Even though they are still viewed as a hardware company, majority of their software revenue comes from subscriptions.

Software also allows easier management of customer accounts and results in renewal opportunities. Cisco has been rolling out enormous improvements to its product offerings because of changing customer requirements.

Cisco ONE is one great case of how Cisco is helping its partners boost their recurring revenue. Cisco ONE comprises of various software suites that provide flexible way for customers to acquire software for their data center, routing, switching and wireless needs in a cost-effective manner. Partners sell a single Cisco ONE software product instead of separately priced software features.

In general, Cisco's product accentuation can be seen over all significant innovation classes, which are planned for making IT basic, for example,

- Cisco Meraki
- Cisco Umbrella
- Cisco WebEx Teams
- Cisco Hyperflex

Car Subscription Service

We live in the future where you're no longer limited to conventional vehicle purchasing and leasing. The traditional methods for getting a car are purchasing and leasing, but car subscription services offer a whole new way of having your own car. Subscription services are targeted to twenty to thirty-year old's and different buyers who need a vehicle yet aren't really keen in ownership.

A subscription gives a driver the chance to drive and switch among various vehicles every year, for a solitary preset value that covers the utilization of the vehicle, and typically insurance, maintenance, licenses, and taxes. The driver just needs to pay for fuel, tolls, and a deductible sum if there is a mishap. It is a good solution for individuals on temporary work movements or others for whom a long-term lease makes no sense or for those who find the ability to drive multiple different models appealing.

Pricing structures vary depending on who offers the service and the types of cars available. There are flat rate plans that placed a new car in your driveway on demand and more flexible plans with fees that change depending on the vehicle you choose and the number of miles you intend to drive in a given month. Below are few benefits of this model.

- The car of your choice is always available at the request of the consumer
- No long term-commitment to vehicle
- Vehicle insurance and maintanance costs are covered

- The user has the ability to cancel their subscription or reinstate their subscription at any time they prefer to do so, much unlike that of any lease program, with the avoidance of any added fees
- Depending on the service, you may be able to swap out your set of wheels for a new one for a relatively small fee, even on short notice
- Car subscription services focus on new cars
- Some of the car subscription services lets you swap out cars as often as every 30 days

Much like with leasing a car, most subscriptions have constraints concerning what number of miles you can drive. A few subscriptions have you pick your mileage toward the beginning of every month and charge as needs be. On the off chance that there's where you don't plan to drive as much not surprisingly, at that point you can drop the mileage down and save money on that month's charges. Then again, in the event that you intend to drive more than ordinary, at that point basically up the mileage for that month and you're secured.

Personalization can help make a good customer experience better.

India's leading utility vehicle manufacturer, Mahindra and Mahindra has come up with a subscription-based passenger car ownership model in partnership with Revv, a car-sharing start-up.

Subscription business model will be available on chosen cars for a time of one to four years. The arrangement incorporates zero initial installment, no street charge, protection, no danger of resale esteem and no upkeep as the month to month fixed sum incorporates every one of these expenses. This plan lets the users change or upgrade the cars they want. They get access to driving a brand-new car under this model.

The subscription business model also represents a shift in how automakers and car buyers view the ownership experience. Several automakers have jumped onto the subscription bandwagon. Car subscription service is here to stay and make a big impact.

To know more details on some of the car subscription services, please visit the below link.

https://www.autoblog.com/car-subscription-services/

Boxycharm Subscription

Boxycharm is one of the most popular beauty subscription boxes we've checked, with a lot of loyal customers. They guarantee 4-5 full-size products of excellence, ranging from makeup and skincare to shading beauty care products, each month from a variety of established brands, with an average retail price of over $100 in each event.

A month-to-month membership costs $21 per month. They offer a rebate if customers pay ahead of time to get Boxycharm for as low as $19.25 every month by prepaying $231 for a yearly membership.

For any business to succeed, it must have enough customers to buy the product or service offered. Boxycharm has worked admirably in assessing the potential customer base and makes sense of the objective customers. What customers love about Boxycharm are listed below.

- Over $100 value in every $21 box
- 4-5 full-sized items every month
- Easy online cancellation process
- Earn points each month and redeem in the Charm Shop for even more products

The products' features vary from month to month and will include beauty tools as well as skincare and haircare items.

For additional details on this topic, please visit the below link.

https://www.boxycharm.com/

Conclusion

Over the last decade, several successful subscription-based businesses have been multiplying year-over-year. "Successful" can hold various meanings from million-dollar companies to profitable small businesses that provide a good living for entrepreneurs. The moment you decide that a subscription-based business is the right business model for your company, ask yourself the following questions:

• Is there a need that my product or service provides a solution for? By talking to customers on a regular basis, you will come to know of their problems. With this, your company can come up with effective solutions for addressing those problems.

• Will my subscription offering provide anything unique compared to my competitors?

• Does my product or service hold more value if offered on a recurring basis?

• Do I have enough funds to invest in customer procurement?

• Do I know the right pricing model that my company needs to effectively run this business?

- How often do I need to access the pricing model and make changes if necessary?

- Is my product susceptible to declining interest of customers?

- Are there vendors I could work with to make my service or product more varied and interesting?

- What features, services, and upgrades can I offer my customers from time to time?

- What are the reward programs for loyal customers and members that I could think of?

- How can I make customers opt for the renewal of services, be it autorenewal or manual renewal at the end of the current term?

- Do I have agents who can help negotiate with customers who are not sure of continuing the service but have thoughts of opting for mid-term cancellations or termination of services?

- What does the survey of customers who quit subscription say? Is there a pattern? Any lessons learnt?

- How often will the performance of my company be measured?

- How is the trend of MRR churn and customer retention rate?

With a good plan and strategy laid out about customer and product growth, a subscription-based model might be a great option for your company!

Printed in Great Britain
by Amazon